DIRT, WATER, STONE

A CENTURY OF PRESERVING MESA VERDE

By

Kathleen Fiero

ISBN 1-887805-19-2

Author
Kathleen Fiero

Mesa Verde Centennial Series Editor
Andrew Gulliford

Content and Copy Editor
Elizabeth A. Green

Design and Layout
Lisa Snider Atchison

Mesa Verde Centennial Series Editorial Committee
Lisa Snider Atchison, Tracey L. Chavis,
Elizabeth A. Green, Andrew Gulliford, Tessy Shirakawa,
Duane A. Smith and Robert Whitson

Printed in Korea

For my husband, Don,

and my dad and mom, Fred and Ruby Wasson.

A message from the Superintendent of Mesa Verde National Park

Our centennial celebrates an important moment in Mesa Verde National Park's history. It is an opportunity to share stories of what led to establishment of the park on June 29, 1906, and its designation as a World Heritage Cultural Site in 1978. This is a time to reflect upon its past and share hopes and visions for the next 100 years.

As Mesa Verde National Park nears its 100th birthday, it is important to remember that the archaeological sites it protects have been here far longer. Their survival is a credit to the skilled Ancestral Puebloan masons who created them 700 to 1600 years ago.

Following the Puebloan people's migration south to the Rio Grande area around 1300, the Utes continued to occupy the Mesa Verde area. They remain today and were responsible for the protection and preservation of Mesa Verde prior to its establishment as a national park. The park and the American public owe much to all these surviving indigenous people.

More than 100 years before its establishment as a national park, non-native people began exploring and documenting the archaeological sites at Mesa Verde, including Spanish explorers, geologists, ranchers, miners, photographers, naturalists, and archaeologists. They shared the story of fantastic stone cities in the cliffs, attracting more and more visitors to the area.

Prior to 1914, the 25-mile trek from Mancos Canyon to Spruce Tree House took an entire day, traveling the first 15 miles by wagon and the next 10 miles on foot or by horseback. This included a nearly vertical climb to the top of Chapin Mesa. Today more than one-half million people visit Mesa Verde National Park each year – a considerable increase over the 100 visitors documented in 1906.

"Leaving the past in place" is just one of the unique ideas pioneered at Mesa Verde. In 1908, when archaeology mainly consisted of collecting artifacts for distant museums, Jesse Walter Fewkes repaired, but did not rebuild, Spruce Tree House for visitation. He documented the excavation and created a small museum to house its artifacts. That tradition is continued today and Mesa Verde is recognized worldwide as a leader in non-invasive archaeology – studying and documenting sites without shovels to disturb the past. With the involvement of the 24 tribes affiliated with Mesa Verde and ongoing research, we continue to learn more about the stories that Mesa Verde National Park preserves.

Our centennial will celebrate 100 years of preservation and honor all who have gone before us. This centennial book series was created to tell some of their stories, of discovery, travel, transportation, archaeology, fire and tourism. These stories have contributed to our national heritage and reinforce why we must continue to preserve and protect this national treasure for future generations.

Enjoy the celebration. Enjoy the book series. Enjoy your national park.

– Larry T. Wiese

About the Mesa Verde Museum Association

Mesa Verde Museum Association (MVMA) is a nonprofit, 501 (c) 3 organization, authorized by Congress, established in 1930, and incorporated in 1960. MVMA was the second "cooperating association" formed in the United States after the Yosemite Association. Since its inception, the museum association has provided information that enables visitors to more fully appreciate the cultural and natural resources in Mesa Verde National Park and the southwestern United States. Working under a memorandum of agreement with the National Park Service, the association assists and supports various research activities, interpretive and education programs, and visitor services at Mesa Verde National Park.

A Board of Directors sets policy and provides guidance for the association. An Executive Director assures mission goals are met, strengthens partnerships, and manages publishing, education, and membership program development. A small year-round staff of five, along with more than 15 seasonal employees, operates four sales outlets in Mesa Verde National Park and a bookstore in Cortez, Colorado. The association carries nearly 600 items, the majority of which are produced by outside vendors. MVMA currently publishes approximately 40 books, videos, and theme-related items, and more than 15 trail guides.

Since 1996 MVMA has been a charter partner in the Plateau Journal, a semi-annual interpretive journal covering the people and places of the Colorado Plateau. In addition, the association has been a driving force in the Peaks, Plateaus & Canyons Association (PPCA), a region-wide conference of nonprofit interpretive associations. PPCA promotes understanding and protection of the Colorado Plateau through the publication of joint projects that are not feasible for smaller associations.

Mesa Verde Museum Association is also a longtime member of the Association of Partners for Public Lands (APPL). This national organization of nonprofit interpretive associations provides national representation with our land management partners and highly specialized training opportunities for board and staff.

Since 1930 the association has donated more than $2 million in cash contributions, interpretive services, and educational material to Mesa Verde National Park. MVMA's goal is to continue enhancing visitor experience through its products and services, supporting vital park programs in interpretation, research and education.

Visit the online bookstore at mesaverde.org and learn more about Mesa Verde National Park's centennial celebration at mesaverde2006.org. Contact MVMA offices for additional information at: telephone 970-529-4445; write P.O. Box 38, Mesa Verde National Park, CO 81330; or email info@mesaverde.org.

The Center of Southwest Studies

The Center of Southwest Studies on the campus of Fort Lewis College in Durango, Colorado, serves as a museum and a research facility, hosts public programs, and strengthens an interdisciplinary Southwest college curriculum. Fort Lewis College offers a four-year degree in Southwest Studies with minors in Native American Studies and Heritage Preservation. The Center includes a 4,400-square-foot gallery, the Robert Delaney Research Library, a 100-seat lyceum, and more than 10,000 square feet of collections storage. The new $8 million Center of Southwest Studies building is unique among four-year public colleges in the West, because the facility houses the departments of Southwest Studies and Anthropology, and the Office of Community Services, which helps Four Corners communities with historic preservation and cultural resource planning.

The Colorado Commission on Higher Education has recognized the Center of Southwest Studies as a "program of excellence" in state-funded higher education. Recent gifts to the Center include the $2.5 million Durango Collection ®, which features more than eight hundred years of southwestern weavings from Pueblo, Navajo and Hispanic cultures.

The goal of the Center is to become the intellectual heart of Durango and the Southwest and to provide a variety of educational and research opportunities for students, residents, scholars and visitors. Strengths in the Center's collections of artifacts include Ancestral Puebloan ceramic vessels, more than 500 textiles and dozens of southwestern baskets. The Center's holdings, which focus on the Four Corners region, include more than 8,000 artifacts, 20,000 volumes, numerous periodicals, and 500 special collections dating from prehistory to the present and with an emphasis on southwestern archaeology, maps, and original documents. These collections include nearly two linear miles of manuscripts, unbound printed materials, more than 7,000 rolls of microfilm (including about 3,000 rolls of historic Southwest region newspapers), 600 oral histories, and 200,000 photographs. Contact the Center at 970-247-7456 or visit the Center's website at swcenter.fortlewis.edu. The Center hosts tours, educational programs, a speakers' series, and changing exhibits throughout the year.

Center of Southwest Studies website: http://swcenter.fortlewis.edu

About the publisher

The publisher for the Mesa Verde Centennial Series is the Ballantine family of Durango and the Durango Herald Small Press. The Ballantine family moved to the Four Corners region in 1952 when they purchased the *Durango Herald* newspaper.

Durango has a magnificent setting, close to the Continental Divide, the 13,000-foot San Juan Mountains, and the 500,000-acre Weminuche Wilderness. The Four Corners region encompasses the juncture of Colorado, Utah, Arizona, and New Mexico, the only place in the nation where four state borders meet. Residents can choose to ski one day in the San Juans and hike the next day in the wilderness canyons of Southeast Utah. This land of mountains and canyons, deserts and rivers is home to diverse Native American tribes including the Southern Utes, Ute Mountain Utes, Jicarilla Apache, Hopi, Zuni, and the Navajo, whose 17-million-acre nation sprawls across all four states. The Four Corners is situated on the edge of the Colorado Plateau, which has more national forests, national parks, national monuments, and wilderness areas than anywhere else on earth.

Writing and editing the newspaper launched countless family expeditions to Ancestral Puebloan sites in the area, including spectacular Mesa Verde National Park, the world's first park set aside for the preservation of cultural resources in 1906 to honor America's indigenous peoples. The Ballantine family, through the *Durango Herald* and the *Cortez Journal,* have been strong supporters of Mesa Verde National Park and Fort Lewis College.

Arthur and Morley Ballantine started the planning for the Center of Southwest Studies at Fort Lewis College in 1964 with a $10,000 gift. In 1994 Morley began the Durango Herald Small Press, which publishes books of local and regional interest. The Press is proud to be a part of the 100th birthday celebration for Mesa Verde National Park.

Durango Herald Small Press website: www.durangoheraldsmallpress.com

ACKNOWLEDGMENTS

First I must thank Beth Green who compressed, eliminated and refined a wordy, often poorly organized manuscript, and Lisa Atchison for adding the glamour. Tracey Chavis of the Mesa Verde Museum Association and Tessy Shirakawa of the National Park Service must also be thanked. They got me into this - six months of reminiscing. It's been fun. Linda Towle, Don Fiero and Andy Gulliford read the manuscript and their comments were much appreciated if not always followed. The staff of the Mesa Verde Research Center helped in finding and scanning photographs and plan maps: Liz Bauer, Carolyn Landes, Patti Bell, Kristen Jones, Linda Martin, Noreen Fritz, Angelyn Rivera, Kathy McKay and Gretchen Gray. Kara Naber helped in locating tree ring data for the various cliff dwellings. Tom Windes was helpful with email messages on the latest in Chaco research. Jenny Barker, a student intern at Mesa Verde from Fort Lewis College, took several of the recent color photographs of the cliff dwellings. Recent research at Mesa Verde has involved the work of many archaeologists. The research on Cliff Palace was directed by Larry Nordby, on Spruce Tree House by Joel Brisbin, and on the kilns by Gay Ives. Joel is now following in my footsteps as the head of the stabilization program. I certainly wish him well and hope he has as enjoyable and fulfilling an experience as I had.

I must also thank those I worked for at Mesa Verde – my supervisors, the park superintendent, the division budget clerk; those I worked with – contractors as well as park staff; and those who worked for me. These last deserve the greatest thanks. They made me look good – at least most of the time. For the successes I must share all credit with them. For the failures – they were mine alone. Being a supervisor has its downside. Very special thanks go to four people who really were instrumental in my success at Mesa Verde. One is Mary Griffitts, geologist extraordinare, friend and the reason for the success (at least up to the time I retired when my responsibility ended) of the preservation techniques used on Square Tower in Hovenweep National Monument. We both are also addicted to reading mysteries and had fun discussing Nevada Barr's various books in that genre. Second, Frank Matero, conservator/teacher, was the man of the hour when it came to the conservation of mud mortars, plasters and the stones in-between. He was great to work with and made a wicked margarita – even with bits of plastic floating in the mix! Sally Cole, rock art specialist/anthropologist, made me re-look at resources I thought I knew – "a bear paw, oh right, I can see it!" And who else could get a lawyer husband to pack a ladder down one of the steepest trails in Mesa Verde? One volunteer, Myers Walker, is responsible for the digital recreations of decorated panels in Long House and Step House. Finally Jeff Dean, tree ring specialist/archaeologist, who by looking at wood and its rings advanced our knowledge of the Mesa Verde cliff dwellings more than anyone since Gustaf Nordenskiöld. And what great dinners we had at Nero's.

Not all was fun and games in the park. I sat back and watched as my supervisor at the time, Jack Smith, put his job on the line to preserve one cliff dwelling, Long House, from the pressure of the recreation/filming industry. He took real heat when he said "no" to the filming of a few frames for the movie "Indiana Jones and the Temple of Doom." Higher ups in the NPS gave the okay – because "there is nothing left to learn from such a cliff dwelling." They were so wrong. Jack really deserves the heartfelt thanks of resource managers everywhere.

I had my downers while at Mesa Verde – and not over such a compelling issue as Jack's. I received two official reprimands, both late in my Mesa Verde career. One was due to my arrogance as a supervisor – I can handle this. Well, I couldn't. Another came when I disobeyed my supervisor to save a wall – at least that was my take. Stressful times for me. Also a third of "our" stabilization shed was taken over by another park group in need. So painful for the crew and me – we proved to be very territorial animals.

But there were also some real high points – the five months I spent studying preservation in Rome would definitely be near the top. But at the very top would be living in a national park. While most people in this country were commuting to work on clogged streets, I walked the mile from home to the stabilization shed. Instead of exhaust fumes I enjoyed clean air, beautiful trees, singing birds, wildflowers, deer, foxes, squirrels, and cicadas. The house we called home dated back to Jesse Nusbaum. The night skies were incredible. It was an hour's drive to the closest mall and a five-hour drive to the closest freeway. Weekends were often spent camping in one of the Four Corners states. All in all it was a fun, challenging, intellectually and physically expanding and demanding 20 years. And it was the people I worked for, worked with, and who worked for me, and the environment where all of this took place that made it so.

TABLE OF CONTENTS

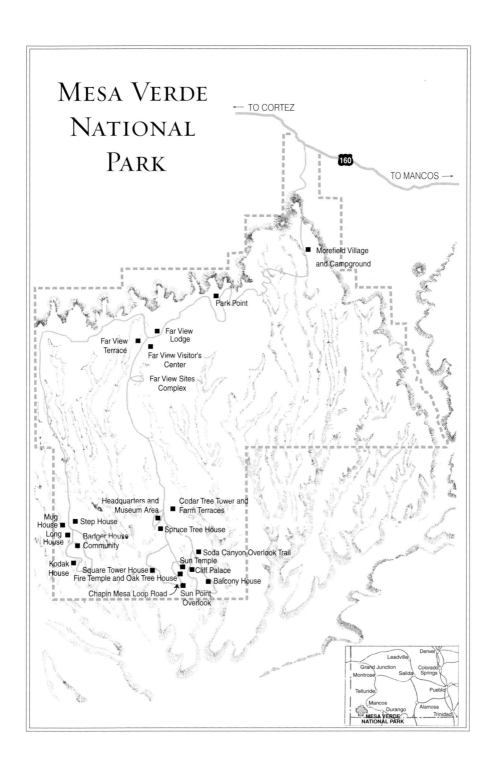

MESA VERDE
NATIONAL
PARK

← TO CORTEZ

160

TO MANCOS →

Morefield Village
and Campground

Park Point

Far View
Lodge

Far View
Terrace

Far View Visitor's
Center

Far View Sites
Complex

Headquarters and
Museum Area

Cedar Tree Tower and
Farm Terraces

Mug
House

Step House

Spruce Tree House

Long
House

Badger House
Community

Soda Canyon Overlook Trail

Kodak
House

Sun Temple

Square Tower House

Cliff Palace

Fire Temple and Oak Tree House

Balcony House

Chapin Mesa Loop Road

Sun Point
Overlook

Denver

Leadville

Grand Junction

Colorado
Springs

Montrose

Salida

Telluride

Pueblo

Mancos

Alamosa

Durango

Trinidad

MESA VERDE
NATIONAL PARK

FOREWORD

November 1986: I'm sitting on a plane and the person next to me asks where I'm from, "southwestern Colorado" and what I do, "I'm an archaeologist."

"What do archaeologists do?"

"Well, you've seen the Indiana Jones movies, haven't you?"

We both laugh.

Then I continue, "I'm in charge of the ruins stabilization program at Mesa Verde National Park."

"I visited Mesa Verde years ago and I still remember what a great place it was. You are sure lucky."

"I am. I can't imagine a better job."

It is a beautiful, clear day with light winds and temperatures in the 70s and 80s. Dressed in special jump suits, we head to the heliport. A few minutes later we land on an isolated finger of Chapin Mesa, the helicopter rotor lifting the dry earth into clouds of dust. We then rappel down ropes into a small cliff dwelling visited only by squirrels and pack rats in the last 100 years. The helicopter soon returns with a barrel of water attached to a long-line and then a short time after that with screened dirt in a barrel on the long-line. The last load is our tools and acrylic polymer, to be mixed with dirt to form mortar used in re-pointing cliff dwelling masonry. That is the romance of the job, an image we use to impress people. It happened maybe 30 times in the 16 seasons I supervised the stabilization crew.

More typically, it is cold (or hot) and breezy, and we use hoes all day to control weeds around and in Far View House, Coyote Village, Sun Temple, Mug House, and other such better known sites. The Navajos on the crew call this type of day "easy money," but most *belagaanas* (Navajo for white men/women) see only boredom. Such days came about 30 times a year - the more typical reality.

The terms stabilization, preservation, and conservation have faded in and out of favor in the past 50 or so years. "Stabilization" was the term used when I first started in the profession. Then "preservation" gained favor and now "conservation" seems to be preferred. Whichever word is applied to it, the job has always been to retain and make stable the standing architecture of archaeological sites. What has changed is the modern emphasis on documenting that architecture prior to any modifications, and then documenting the changes made in the intervention process. Being an old-timer, I will use the term "stabilization," but in an inclusive way referring to documentation as well as direct intervention.

Archaeological sites are preserved for two reasons: to save information and to teach others about them. Each site is like a book that hasn't been opened. It contains information about the people who built and lived there, whether it was a village, house, campground, or something else. Like a book, you don't want to destroy it before it is investigated. These villages are also important as educational tools. Once stabilized, they can be opened to visitation so the public can learn about the people who once lived in these places.

If a site is relatively stable – and there are many of these in Mesa Verde National Park – nothing more is done except to make sure it remains stable. The roofs and walls that once were part of mesa top or canyon villages collapsed long ago. These areas – often mounds and depressions – are covered with wind-blown soil and shrubs and typically disturbed only by wildfires and major flooding. Villages or other features located on unstable terrain can be a problem, but for the most part these open sites have become fairly stable in the past 700 or more years, and are not a major stabilization concern.

Stabilization work focuses on the 600 or so cliff dwellings and a few sites with standing walls situated on the mesa top and canyon floors. Some that are not visited by the public need to be monitored for potential problems – walls that are being undercut or driplines that are forcing runoff water onto structures. If the condition threatens a wall or feature in the dwelling, stabilization measures are undertaken. The goal is to make the wall or feature stable with minimal impact to the scientific information contained in the site. Among those who are trained to preserve artifacts and architecture, the guiding principle stipulates they should not do anything that cannot be easily reversed.

Then there are those sites that visitors enter or view from afar. This category includes sites that have been excavated for the purpose of visitor education and include such spectacular villages as Cliff Palace and Long House, but also Square Tower House and Oak Tree House and the mesa top sites of Far View House and Twin Trees Community and Badger House Community. There are a wide range of village types: from pithouses to jacal-walled rooms to cliff dwellings. These are the resources on which the stabilization crew spends most of its time and energy.

From 1986 to 2002 I supervised the stabilization program in Mesa Verde National Park. I followed in the footsteps of Jesse Walter Fewkes and Jesse Nusbaum who, as outside contractors in the early years of the park, excavated and stabilized the major cliff dwellings. But it was National Park Service employees Al Lancaster (1934-64), Al Decker (1964-80), and Ron Crawford (1980-86) whose shoes I would have to fill. They had hired the crew I supervised for much of my stay, and set the schedule of work as well as the techniques used. I would be constantly grateful to them in my 16-year supervisory career at Mesa Verde. I put in many years of working on or with the crew before I felt comfortable making amendments to that schedule, modifying techniques, or adapting new materials.

I came to this job with a background in field archaeology. Before moving to Mesa Verde in 1982, I had never given a second thought to preserving the archaeological record. My interest was in excavating sites for what I could learn from them, but not in preserving them afterward. In my four years of seasonal work at Mesa Verde, from 1983 to mid-1986, I was exposed to the concept of preservation and had practical experience supervising a seasonal crew that was stabilizing Far View House. Then in mid-season 1986, when Ron Crawford left, I was asked to step in as supervisor of the park's stabilization program. Little did I realize then what a defining moment this would be for me and my career.

– Kathleen Fiero
Santa Fe, New Mexico
Summer 2005

I

The Mesa
and its People

Looking south from Far View.

Jenny L. Barker

I n the 13th century some farmers in the northern part of the
American Southwest took an unusual step. They decided to move
into cliff-face alcoves to build their homes and religious architecture.
These farmers, whose ancestors had been living on mesa tops and in broad
canyons and valleys for centuries, are the ancestors of the Pueblo Indians of
Arizona and New Mexico. In a matter of a few generations, they built habitation rooms and ceremonial architecture, modified them, and then abandoned
them. By the end of the 13th century, construction had stopped.

Mesa Verde National Park was set aside to preserve and interpret a small
percentage of the hundreds of these cliff dwellings found in the northern
Southwest, including some of the best preserved and largest of such structures. National park status has led to special responsibilities for balancing
the preservation of these very fragile resources with the public's desire for
access to them. This is the National Park Service's mandate and the challenge of the stabilization crew.

THE PLACE

Mesa Verde National Park is located in southwestern Colorado and
includes only a portion of the cuesta named Mesa Verde, or green table-

land, by early Spaniards. The Ute Mountain Tribal Park covers much of the rest of the mesa, which is drained by canyons that divide it into numerous long, narrow fingers. In the national park, those fingers include Wetherill Mesa on the very western side of the park, Long Mesa, and Chapin Mesa, which is near the center and contains the park's main resources: Cliff Palace, Spruce Tree House, and Balcony House as well as the museum, administration building, and the stabilization crew's "office." The Far View area, where the visitor center is located, is at the very north end of Chapin Mesa. From there a panoramic view can be seen of not only Chapin Mesa but the whole Mesa Verde landform, as well as Shiprock to the south, Sleeping Ute Mountain to the west, and the La Plata Mountains to the east.

In the park's semiarid climate, pinyon and juniper are the dominant plants on the mesa top, as is sage on the canyon floors. Gambel oak is predominant at higher elevations within the park. With an average elevation of approximately 7,000 feet, the mesa slopes to the south. The north escarpment is over 8,000 feet and the lowest canyon floors and the south end of the mesa are under 6,000 feet. The park receives approximately 18 inches of precipitation annually but this varies widely from year to year, from less than 10 inches to more than 30 inches. The frost-free period is typically from late May to early November. Precipitation falls as snow in the winter and as rain from violent thunderstorms in late summer. The growing season averages 158 days but can vary widely. The driest months are January and June – with January also the coldest and June one of the hottest.

The weather is quite variable. Raymond, a longtime member of the stabilization crew, often commented that he had seen snow falling every month of the year.

Deep intermittent streams drain the cuesta, and flow into the Mancos River, a permanently flowing stream several miles south of the park's major cliff dwellings. Stream erosion has cut the mesa into numerous roughly parallel, north-south-trending and southward-dipping fingers. Permanent seeps and springs are found within the park at the contact of sandstone and shale geologic beds and – along with rain – were the source of water for the village occupants.

THE PEOPLE

The village people of Mesa Verde were typical of desert farmers the world over – conservative, religious, family-oriented, and obsessed with weather and water. Change came slowly. With little access to trade goods, they had to rely on their own skills – cutting trees, shaping stone, making and decorating pottery, building walls and roofs, growing corn, beans, and squash, hunting deer and rabbits, raising turkeys for their feathers and meat, gathering wild seeds, roots, and leaves for food and medicine, and praying for rain and a good harvest. They married, gave birth, raised a family, and died – probably all within a few miles of where they were born. The skills displayed in the architecture and material culture of these people are those that could be expected of every person of a certain sex and age. There was no specialization of work beyond those associated with age and gender. They learned the things that all of us today would learn if we were raised in such an environment – if we lived in a cliff dwelling all our lives, we would have no fear of heights.

It's a tribute to us as a species that such ordinary people created such beauty in their clustering of buildings and in the designs on their pottery. What language did they speak? Undoubtedly it was an ancient version of one of the Pueblo languages – Hopi, Zuni, Keres – or one of the Tanoan languages – Tewa, Tiwa or Towa. Zuni and Keres are both unique languages with no close relatives in Native America. Hopi is a member of one of the largest language families in North America – the UtoAztecan language family – and Tanoan is also related to a number of other North American languages. DNA has established that the people of the Northern San Juan were genetically of the same population as modern Pueblo Indians.

The Mesa Verdean men were on average 5 feet 4 inches tall and the women 5 feet. A one-year-old male child could expect to live another 25 years and a female child 20 years. There was a high mortality rate for infants, adolescents and women in their reproductive years. A little more than 11 percent of the population lived to be over 40 years old. They were fairly healthy, at least on the evidence remaining from their bones and, for people living in cliffs, had surprisingly few broken bones. About 85 percent of the population had deformed heads, due to babies being attached firmly to cradle boards. Such flattened skulls were undoubtedly desired, considered attractive.

TIME AND SPACE

The Mesa Verde landform extends beyond the national park boundaries and is, in turn, surrounded by a much bigger area with very similar archaeological sites. This greater area, the Northern San Juan, encompasses the area from the San Juan River to the Dolores River, and from Durango, Colorado, to Cedar Mesa in eastern Utah. The farming people of this larger area were all cultivating similar plants, creating similar pottery shapes and designs, and building similar religious architecture. Other culture areas are the Kayenta, southwest of Mesa Verde in Arizona, and Chaco, southeast of Mesa Verde in the central San Juan Basin. Architecture and ceramic styles distinguish the three areas but the similarities are so great that they are considered one cultural tradition, the Ancestral Pueblo/Anasazi.

People in each major area focused their creativity on different aspects of their material goods. The Chaco people were obsessed with architecture. Once seen it can never be forgotten. The Kayenta people were the greatest potters of their time period on the Colorado Plateau. Mesa Verde pots from the 13th century are beautiful; Kayenta pots from the same time period are incredible. And anyone who set foot in what is now Utah seemed to focus on the beautiful sandstone and created remarkable rock art.

PECOS CLASSIFICATION SYSTEM

PaleoIndian 8000-6000BC
Archaic 6000-1000BC
Basketmaker II (BMII) 1000BC-AD500
Basketmaker III (BMIII) AD500-750
Pueblo I (PI) AD750-900
Pueblo II (PII) AD900-1150
Pueblo III (PIII) AD1150-1300
Pueblo IV (PIV) AD1300-1540
Pueblo V (PV) AD1540-present

The concentration of rock art in Chaco, Mesa Verde, or the Kayenta area is minimal compared to the area north of the San Juan River and west of Sleeping Ute Mountain. Interestingly, the Mesa Verdeans had no special obsession, no real outstanding objects. They were generalists who lived in a stunning landscape that they in part created out of their construction practices.

Both the Northern San Juan and the Kayenta subareas are known for their 13th century cliff dwellings. The Chaco area is known for its spectacular 11th and 12th century standing architecture. In both the Kayenta and Northern San Juan, only a percentage of the cliff dwellings were built in alcoves and on ledges that demanded extraordinary means for entry – long ladders, ropes, and such. In Mesa Verde, probably more than 90 percent of the rooms built in alcoves and on ledges are relatively easy to enter. But some rooms and clusters of rooms were definitely built in hard-to-reach locations. Even with a helicopter, fancy climbing ropes, and 40-foot extension ladders, some sites in the park are a challenge to enter. Balcony House is certainly not one of the most difficult, but it is the most difficult of those that are open to the public and there is no question that those who built it wanted access to be a challenge.

Not only have archaeologists divided the landscape into several areas on the basis of the similarity of material culture attributes, but they have also divided Pueblo prehistory into several periods with the objective of organizing data into more manageable packages. Through time, people – and the things they use and create – change, sometimes more rapidly than others. Sometimes change occurs in one area of material culture and not in another. Grinding stones, for example, stayed much the same through long periods whereas pottery designs changed quite rapidly. But change is inevitable and to break this timeline into manageable bits, period names have been established.

The most widely used system evolved out of an early Pecos Conference, and so it is called the Pecos classification system.

A Basketmaker I period was created on the assumption that something before the earliest then known agricultural period would appear. In fact, this period of early experimentation with cultivating plants is now referred to as late Archaic, so the Basketmaker I name has never been used for a period.

TREE RING RESEARCH

All early archaeologists were deeply frustrated by their inability to place their observations in real time: When was Cliff Palace occupied? For how long? And was it before or after the occupation of such sites as Aztec Ruins and Pueblo Bonito in New Mexico, and Spruce Tree House and Oak Tree House in Mesa Verde? Mesa Verde was only a peripheral player in the drive to develop a tree ring sequence that could be used to answer such questions. But dating is so important to an understanding of Mesa Verde prehistory that a word on tree ring dating is in order.

As early as 1904, the astronomer A.E. Douglas began to look more closely at tree rings and dating, noting that rings varied in size. He figured out that he could go back in time by matching ring size clusters. Rings of many trees vary based on the amount of moisture received during the growing period. Since the sequence of wet and dry years varies through time, the year a tree was cut (cutting date) can be determined once a master chronology for an area is created. In less than 20 years from the initial collection of prehistoric and historic wood samples, a real-time chronology covering Pueblo prehistory was developed. Those were frustrating years for southwestern archaeologists. Mesa Verde was included in the flurry of sampling in the '20s to find wood that would extend and finally bridge the gap in the historic and prehistoric sequences, but finally in 1929 the gap was filled from a site in Arizona. Once that was done, the Mesa Verde cliff dwellings with structural, datable wood could be dated – 13th century.

There are, of course, problems with jumping from a cutting date on a piece of structural wood, and a construction date for the room. After all, wood can be reused; trees can be cut well before use; and a wood member can be replaced without the whole room being rebuilt. But with care and multiple dates for a room, a year and even the season for construction can be established. Because of the common occurrence of datable wood in archaeological sites on the Colorado Plateau, this area is blessed with one of the highest rates of firmly dated archaeological sites in the world. And, of course once the wood is dated, then the accompanying pottery, projectile points, and ground stone can be dated. When those same types of artifacts are found on sites without datable wood, the assumption can be made that the site is of similar age.

EARLY TREE RING RESEARCH

In the early years of tree ring dating, the concern was to date as many sites as possible in order to compare architecture and other aspects of material culture across a wide area. More recently the focus has been on dating as many samples from a particular village as possible. The objective now is to better understand and date the growth and modifications to a particular village through time.

2

PITHOUSE TO PUEBLO: AD600 TO 1300 ON THE MESA

Cliff Palace before repair, 1900.

Winter 1984-85: I am skiing along the Cliff Palace loop road and, as I often do, take off my skis and go to the overlook to gaze down on Cliff Palace. What I see is unforgettable: a group of bighorn sheep on the trail in front of the site, browsing on vegetation. A young sheep is gazing into a front kiva. Cliff dwellings are compelling to all sorts of mammals, not just humans.

F or thousands of years after people entered the Americas, there is no evidence of anyone living on Mesa Verde: no big game hunters, hunters and gatherers, or early farmers. Then between 600 and 1300, Mesa Verde experienced an explosion of occupation that has never been rivaled – and this by a group of small-scale farmers who relied on rainwater for their crops, springs for drinking water, corn as the staff of life, and villages to support their economic, religious, and social needs. Their dwellings evolved from pithouses to pueblos. In the 13th century these farm families moved into natural alcoves found in cliffs, but within a century all construction stopped and residents left. After 1300 it was quiet again on Mesa Verde, for another 600 years. There is no evidence of permanent occupation until Park Superintendent Nusbaum and his family moved onto the mesa in 1922.

During the 700 years that Mesa Verde was home to ancestors of the Pueblo Indians of Arizona and New Mexico, their homes and religious architecture, check dams and field houses dotted the landscape. They used natural alcoves found in the mesa cliffs throughout this period. Springs in the alcoves supplied drinking water; overhangs gave protection from the elements; protected expanses of sandstone provided a place to draw figures; and open floors and loose fill were a great place to build homes and religious architecture. For the final 100 years of this occupation, these alcoves became the primary location of villages containing domestic and religious architecture, courtyards, and towers.

"MESA VERDE NATIONAL PARK WAS SET ASIDE TO PRESERVE A CONCENTRATED, YET SMALL, PERCENTAGE OF CLIFF DWELLINGS."

Thirteenth century cliff dwellings are found in many canyons on the Colorado Plateau, an area that stretches in an arc from the Mesa Verde on the east across the canyon country of Utah on the north and ending in the Tsegi Canyon area of Arizona on the west. Mesa Verde National Park was set aside to preserve a concentrated, yet small, percentage of cliff dwellings. Recent tree ring dating makes it clear that, at least in Mesa Verde National Park, this cliff dwelling period was relatively short, 1180-1280, with any one cliff dwelling built over an even shorter span, often less than 50 years. Around 1280 all construction stopped. After farming the area for 700 years, residents left, moving south and southeast to areas more central to the Pueblo world at that time. Although always on the periphery of the Pueblo world, Mesa Verde's outstanding preservation, the size and complexity of the built environment and the aesthetic appeal of the cliff dwellings make it and the national park central to the interpretation of this pre-historic Pueblo world. The result of their cliff dwelling settlement pattern has been standing architecture protected from rain and snow, walls that still retain the original earthen plaster, the original yucca door loops, even finger prints of the 13th century masons who built the walls.

The earliest tree ring dates on the Mesa Verde are from pithouse villages, clusters of semi-subterranean pithouses associated with outdoor storage units, hearths and work areas. Through time this type of housing arrangement was replaced by contiguous above-ground blocks of rooms used for storage and habitation and associated with subterranean ceremonial structures called kivas. Jacal and stone slab construction gave way eventually to

TIME LINE

Semi-nomadic	Pit houses	Single-story villages	Multi-story villages	Cliff dwellings & Mesa top villages	Migration
A.D. 1	A.D. 550	A.D. 750	A.D. 1100	A.D. 1200	A.D. 1300

shaped-stone construction. The plastered earthen pithouse evolved into the stone-lined and plastered kiva. The curved row of storage and habitation rooms became the U-shaped unit pueblo made up of habitation and storage rooms, with a kiva in the central courtyard.

At the beginning of the 13th century, people continued to build unit pueblos but built them as units of larger villages. This type of aggregation is found not just in the cliff dwellings of Mesa Verde but in all the surrounding areas. In the Montezuma Valley to the north of Mesa Verde and Cajon Mesa to the west, such sites are located at the heads of canyons where there are dependable springs, such as the sites preserved in Hovenweep National Monument. To the south the Chacoan sites were restructured to contain smaller rooms and the Mesa Verde style of kiva. Many small villages continued to be built but the overall trend was toward the construction of larger villages. Why this occurred in the 13th century is much debated. Defense and concerns about water and land ownership are the current hypotheses. By the 13th century most of these unit pueblos in Mesa Verde were located individually and in clusters in the natural alcoves, the villages that have come to be called cliff dwellings.

Through their seven centuries on the Mesa Verde, these people relied on growing corn, beans and squash, collecting native plants, and hunting such animals as deer and rabbit for their livelihood. They had domesticated dogs and turkeys. They used native materials such as stone, wood and clay not only to build their homes but also to create beautiful objects for daily use: baskets, pots, and bone and stone tools. Long-distance trade goods such as shell, turquoise, and obsidian were uncommon but design styles for pottery, basketry, rock art, and architecture found on Mesa Verde were common to people living all over the Northern San Juan drainage. This suggests that the people on the Mesa Verde were not dependent on long-distance trade but also did not live in complete isolation. They had some communication with villages in the surrounding area.

Through this whole sequence, the basic unit of construction and social organization was the household. Site size varied, with small single-family sites as well as multi-family units. Besides these typical habitation sites, special purpose sites are also found. Circular subterranean great kivas were associated with clusters of dwellings as early as the pithouse period. Water control features are poorly dated but pervasive across the Mesa Verde: check dams in drainages, rock-lined terraces, and possibly as early as 1100, water reservoirs.

At the time of the Chaco phenomenon to the south (900 to 1100), several large pueblos were constructed at a high, commanding elevation in the Northern San Juan area. Far View House is an excavated example in the park with features that suggest Chaco influence. Far View House is not well dated, since it was excavated before the technique of tree ring dating was developed. But the dates that do exist suggest that construction took place between 900 and 1150 with some activity into the 13th century. Towers associated with kivas were built in isolated units and as part of larger pueblos by 1000 and became a hallmark of the cliff dwelling period on the Northern San Juan. At the time of the cliff dwellings, at least two large rectangular open spaces, defined on either end by massive two-story room blocks, were constructed in alcoves (Long House, Fire Temple) and the D-shaped planned structure known as Sun Temple was built.

In Mesa Verde the 13th century cliff dwellings (more appropriately "alcove village" but the term "cliff dwelling" has been in the literature for over 100 years and will be used here) are almost all located in alcoves, on ledges and in crevices of the upper Cliff House Sandstone Formation. The alcoves were created through natural erosion by physical and chemical weathering. Some of these occupied alcoves and ledges appear defensive because they are very difficult to enter. Others are located at the top of talus with relatively easy access. Many but not all of the alcoves contain springs.

The cliff dwellings vary in size from one-room structures of less than one square meter to complex, multi-storied structures covering over a hundred square meters. The function of rooms ranges from storage to ceremonial, food preparation to sleeping, and many rooms vary in function through time. There are approximately 600 cliff dwellings in Mesa Verde National Park and many more on Ute Mountain Ute tribal lands to the west and south. Of the cliff dwellings in Mesa Verde National Park, well over a quarter contain just one room and over 80 percent contain no more than 10 rooms. Only three sites have more than 100 rooms: Cliff Palace, Long House, and Spruce Tree House. The orientation of the cliff dwellings varies but the majority of them face either west or east, with a few facing south and some even facing north.

The preference (possibly more accurately compulsion) which led to the cliff dwelling type of settlement pattern is not understood. Hypotheses, which have changed as often as the political and intellectual climate in this country, include defense, solar collection, preservation, ownership of drinking water (springs), aesthetics, and architectural fashion. It's not surprising that at this time in our country's history, defense is the most popular explanation, as it was in the early 20th century. But decisions that affect many people almost always have multiple causes and this was probably the case in 13th century Mesa Verde. Many dwellings, such as Spruce Tree House and Mug House, are not difficult to enter. For those that are more of a challenge, such as Balcony House, this restricted access does nothing but trap individuals in their homes and limit visibility. If defense were a factor, they were only defending themselves from other Pueblo Indians, as there is no evidence of Ute or Navajo presence in the area until several centuries later. A few cliff dwellings are perfectly located to capture sun in the winter and shade in the summer – Long House, Fire Temple, and Oak Tree House. But most cliff dwellings face either east or west, making them cold in the winter and only pleasant half of a hot summer day. Cold air drainage in the canyons makes some dwellings, like Spruce Tree House, particularly cold in the winter.

The cliff dwellings were built of local sandstone that was typically chipped and pecked into finished shape. The stone blocks were then set in an earthen mortar. There are a few jacal walls and a few dry-laid sandstone walls. Sandstone boulders and big slabs were incorporated into some walls and there are even a few examples of hand-shaped adobe walls. Standing walls vary from one to two stones wide. The typical room wall was built on a natural or constructed surface above the level of the ground. Kivas were typically built below the ground surface or fill was added around these structures to maintain the appearance of being subsurface. Kiva roofs were incorporated into the floor of a courtyard with rooms and work areas surrounding the kiva-courtyard complex. The walls of kivas were stone-lined with either fill or undisturbed stone or soil behind these walls.

Rooms can have multiple stories, often with the walls of the upper room plastered and the walls of the lower room left without a plaster coat. Floors can be natural (stone or dirt) or mud plaster over either stone or dirt. In multi-storied room blocks, the floor of the upper story is the roof of the lower room. In these cases the floor is wood with one or two primary beams, multiple secondary beams perpendicular to the primaries, and tertiaries of even smaller wood. Juniper bark was used as closing material and then the floor was finished with mortar or paving stones with mortar. Roofs are either the natural roof of the alcove or the wood and mortar construction of floors. The only structures with a different style of roof are kivas, which commonly have cribbed wood roofs with the roofs supported by pilasters.

The layout of cliff dwellings varies tremendously but there are a few standard characteristics. Courtyards with their subsurface kivas are typically outlined on two or three sides with rooms. The bigger cliff dwellings contain several courtyards. Rooms were added and removed through time with little evidence of preplanning at the courtyard level. Some of the larger cliff dwellings have circular rooms (towers) or massive walls at either end of the alcove. Mug House has a tower at both the north and south ends of the site.

Late in the history of many of the larger cliff dwellings, a large wall or other restriction was created, dividing the village into two parts and preventing easy access between them. Multiple courtyards are associated with each half. Many archaeologists assume that this divided architectural space is the result of a socially divided group – possibly the clans clustered into moieties as is found in most Pueblo villages today. Cliff Palace, Long House, Spruce Tree House, Square Tower House, and Oak Tree House are examples of cliff dwellings where access is restricted between two portions of the site.

The other constant topic for debate in southwestern archaeology is the movement of all Pueblo people away from the northern Southwest. From the year 1 to 1280 Pueblo farmers moved into and out of river drainages and uplands on the Colorado Plateau, but the general area was always occupied. Their movement was necessitated by changing weather patterns, soil exhaustion, and overcrowding, and was modified when they improved water management with check dams and terracing, and planted corn that was better adapted to the dry upland environment. As an example, in Mesa Verde the canyons on the east side of the park were more heavily occupied between 900 and 1075, and then in the 13th century, occupation became concentrated in the alcoves on the west side of what is now the park. But then around 1280, occupation of the entire area north of the San Juan

---

... MORE PEOPLE LIVED IN SOUTHWEST COLORADO IN THE 13TH CENTURY THAN DID WHEN MESA VERDE NATIONAL PARK WAS FOUNDED.

River ceased entirely.

In the 14th century large inward-oriented villages were built well south of the San Juan River by ancestors of Pueblo Indians. The kiva-tower-tunnel complex, the Mesa Verde keyhole-shaped kiva, and the courtyard unit all disappeared from the architectural record. They are not found in any modern Pueblo village or in ancestral Pueblo villages dating after the 14th century. Suites and the dual division are found in modern Pueblos but small kivas associated with a cluster of habitation and storage rooms are not. The driving force behind all of these dramatic changes was probably a complex of environmental, social and religious pressures that ripped apart the world as these people knew it.

In the Americas, the collapse of population centers is not unique to the northern San Juan. The Chaco/central San Juan Basin population centers were abandoned somewhat earlier and the Gila and Salt river drainages in southern Arizona somewhat later. Looking farther afield, the Cahokia population center, located along the Mississippi in what is now southwestern Illinois, folded around 1250 and the Maya collapse occurred around 900. The underlying causes of each of these collapses are hotly debated. In the Mesa Verde area it is clear that the late 13th century was a time of diminished rainfall (not that this was unique – drier periods had occurred in the past with no abandonment of the whole area) and populations concentrated into large villages. After this period, the Mesa Verde area was empty while areas that had previously been only sparsely populated became the location of large Pueblo villages – the area around the Rio Chama and Rio Grande, and the Zuni and Hopi areas.

Maybe, in fact, we should be more surprised that pre-Industrial Revolution farming people were able to survive in such an environment as Mesa Verde for as long as they did with only 18 inches of precipitation in an average year and a growing season of 158 days. In an environment marginal for farming, it wouldn't take much to push farmers over the edge – reduced rainfall, a growing season shortened by late or early cold spells, reduced soil fertility, population pressures, dropping water table, erosion, and forest depletion. There are so many things that can go wrong. It is interesting that more people lived in Southwest Colorado in the 13th century than did when Mesa Verde National Park was founded, even with such additions as railroads, water wells, and horses, sheep, and cows. Of course early 20th century Americans demanded more, with their higher standard of living, but still this says a lot about the ability of these early farmers to wrest a living out of their environment. Today, the water people drink in Mesa Verde comes through a pipe that starts northeast of Mancos in the La Plata Mountains. Except for a few employee vegetable gardens, no agricultural products are produced on the mesa now.

For many years the park had a corn plot in an open area off the Cliff Palace loop road, planted and tended by the stabilization crew. This experiment was discontinued due to parking problems before my time but Raymond Begay (stabilization crew foreman) told me that in many years water had to be added to save the crop. I was a very frustrated vegetable gardener in Mesa Verde and I watered regularly. Tomatoes were just getting ripe when the first frost arrived. Cherry tomatoes, zucchini, and raspberries were great. I didn't try corn. Most modern sweet corns demand a much longer growing season than is normal at Mesa Verde.

3

ONE HUNDRED YEARS
OF PRESERVATION:
FEWKES TO FIERO

July 1986: Raymond is reminiscing about what a tough boss Al Lancaster was, saying with obvious admiration for the man and his style: "We started work on the sites at 8 a.m. I can remember being late one day when we were working on Sun Temple and Lancaster drove the wrong way on the Mesa Top Loop. He insisted on being on time. We also had to ask for permission to go to the bathroom. Other times Lancaster would say, 'Don't make a nice wall.' He wanted the new work to look 'Anasazi'."

* * *

April 1987: Spruce Tree House: Raymond and I are looking at a depression in the trail deep enough to trip visitors. He makes his recommendation on what we need to do. I ask a few questions. In his response, Raymond recommends certain repairs and then says something I will hear many times in the following years: "That is how Lancaster did it."

INTRODUCTION

D irt (*slish*), water (*to*), stone (*tse*) – it is amazing what can be produced from such basic materials. They are what the ancestors of the Pueblo Indians used to build Balcony House, Cliff Palace, and the other extraordinary structures in the Southwest, and they are what we use today to maintain them.

Mesa Verde National Park was the first site placed on the UNESCO list of World Cultural Heritage Sites. The list includes such compelling places as the Pyramids of Egypt and the Parthenon of Greece. Not bad for an obscure corner of the Pueblo world and a thinly populated corner of modern-day Colorado. How did this renown come about?

The very early history of Mesa Verde gives no hint of the fame to come. This was Ute Indian country in the 18th century. Utes had been in the region for several centuries and were very familiar with its resources. No definitively Ute artifacts have been recovered from the park but there is extensive documentary evidence of their presence.

Possibly Spanish or Mexican sheepherders gave the name "Mesa Verde" to the landform. The date for this is lost to history. In 1776 the Dominquez-Escalante expedition was in the area and saw ruins to the north but they made no mention of Mesa Verde. The area was explored by EuroAmericans in the 19th century. In 1874 William H. Jackson of the Hayden Survey took the first photograph of a Mesa Verde cliff dwelling, Two Story Cliff House to the south of what would become Mesa Verde National Park, on Ute land overlooking the Mancos River.

The earliest firm evidence of exploration in the park is from 1884, when a group of miners led by S.E. Osborn and including W.H. Hayes wrote their names in Hemenway House and Balcony House. Both sites are

The Wetherill brothers, from left, Al, Winslow, Richard, Clayton and John.

in Soda Canyon, one of Mesa Verde's main drainages on the north side of the Mancos River. They undoubtedly explored down the Mancos River and then up Soda Canyon – the route of many early explorers. But it really wasn't until 1888, when Wetherill family members discovered Cliff Palace and then almost immediately Spruce Tree House, Square Tower House, and other cliff dwellings in that vicinity that word got out about the villages in the cliffs. The Wetherills, who were ranchers in nearby Mancos, were obviously captivated by the villages, and particularly their contents. It looked as if the occupants had just packed up and left – pots, sandals, and baskets were all in place. But of course 1888 was not particularly early for the discovery of Indian ruins. By then many pre-contact sites were known in the Southwest and all over North America.

By 1890 virtually all of the larger cliff dwellings and many of the smaller ones had been visited. Many early explorers removed easily portable objects – from burials to whole pots, baskets to turkey feather blankets – and either sold the objects to interested museums or added them to personal collections. The practice seems to have been accepted by the local and professional community until one collection was sent abroad. A natural scientist from Sweden, Gustaf Nordenskiöld, became so interested in the cliff dwellings in 1891 that with the help and support of the Wetherill family, he excavated and collected objects in several sites. Much of his work was concentrated on Wetherill Mesa, which he named after his supporters. When he tried to send his collection to Sweden, there was a public outcry. Nevertheless, it was legal.

Mesa Verde National Park

Gustaf Nordenskiöld

Ironically, the uproar was directed at a scientist who documented what he removed, unlike locals who had been removing objects for several years with no apparent problem. Nordenskiöld was the single early explorer with a scientific background and took extensive notes on his work. He published the results of his research and excavations, *The Cliff Dwellers of the Mesa Verde*, in 1893, one of the first scientific studies of North American archaeological sites. More than a century later, it contains information still relevant to Mesa Verde archaeology. He speculated that deposits containing pottery in Step House might predate the cliff dwelling period – so realizing the value of chronology, stratigraphy, and culture change, all keys to understanding the past through excavation. But his sending artifacts abroad infuriated the public and became a significant factor in passage of the Antiquities Act 15 years later, on June 8, 1906. The act made "pothunting" on federal lands illegal. Just three weeks later, on June 29, Congress passed the bill creating Mesa Verde National Park. Formation of the park was due to the efforts of such people as Edgar L. Hewett, of the Archaeological Institute of America in New Mexico, and Virginia McClurg and Lucy Peabody of the Colorado Cliff Dwellings Association, who skillfully used the loss of objects to Europe to accomplish their goal, the preservation of antiquities in general and Mesa Verde in particular.

The critical moments in Mesa Verde history came in the early 20th century. First was the passion shown by Hewett and the Colorado Cliff Dwellings Association for preservation of the cliff dwellings following years of looting, from at least 1884 to 1906. Mesa Verde National Park was not the first area in the Southwest set aside for its cultural resources. Arizona's Casa Grande was preserved earlier and the land on which Goodman Point

Mesa Verde National Park

Dr. Jesse Walter Fewkes standing in front of the Chapin Mesa archaeology museum.

Pueblo north of Cortez is located had been removed from homesteading in the late 19th century. But Mesa Verde would become the most famous.

Two other critical variables were Jesse W. Fewkes and Superintendent Jesse L. Nusbaum. Right after the formation of the park, Fewkes readied the sites for interpretation. He created the profession of stabilization and set the standards for the presentation of ruins: cleaned up, stabilized and with their integrity preserved. Between 1908 and 1922 he excavated and stabilized 16 ruins in Mesa Verde National Park – including some of Mesa Verde's most famous villages. He also gave the park service's first campfire programs and established the first museum in the National Park Service.

The third turning point in the park's history took place in 1921 when Jesse Nusbaum was appointed superintendent. After the founding of the park in 1906, political patronage influenced selection of superintendents. In fact, one superintendent's son-in-law spent his free time – from his paid position as park ranger – removing artifacts from the cliff dwellings. Fewkes complained about the practice, and to the right person, the director of the National Park Service, Stephen T. Mather. The director then appointed Nusbaum superintendent, a position he held for over 17 years: 1921-1931, 1936-1939, and 1942-1946.

Nusbaum was the first person to live on the mesa year-round since 1280, when the ancestors of the Pueblo Indians left the area. He camped out the first year, 1921, and then built a permanent residence (still the home of the park superintendent) in a style of architecture that he established, known as Pueblo Revival. Over the next several years, he built a museum, administration building, hospital, natural history museum, and other park housing in the same style – all part of

From left: Dewitt G. Wilcox, ranger, Jesse Nusbaum, superintendent, and Deric Nusbaum, his son, in the summer of 1929.

the museum/administration complex on the mesa across from Spruce Tree House. He schmoozed J.D. Rockefeller, Jr. (who visited the park in 1924) and others, into helping him complete his vision for the park. He filled the new museum with artifacts he collected while excavating in the park. He moved Fewkes' early log museum building and built a new stone structure. Also critical for the establishment of the park as a vacation and education destination, the road into the park was upgraded, even if it was a scary one, during the early years of his administration.

So Hewett and the Cliff Dwellings Association established the park, Fewkes set the stage for the park's approach to the preservation of its cultural resources, their stabilization and interpretation, and Superintendent Nusbaum created a real showcase, building the infrastructure that would meet the needs of the visiting public. It is the Fewkes factor, and how the concern for the techniques and objectives of stabilization developed and changed through the first 100 years of the park's history, that will be emphasized in the following chapters.

FEWKES TO FIERO
The Fewkes Years, 1908-1922: Initial Excavation and Stabilization

Between 1908 and 1922 the ruins for which Mesa Verde is rightfully famous were excavated and stabilized. Most of the work was done by Jesse Walter Fewkes of the Bureau of American Ethnology, under contract to the Department of the Interior, and after 1916 to the newly created

Cliff Palace ca. 1917.
Top: Superintendent Thomas Rickner; Middle: Roger Toll; Lower left to right: unknown,
NPS Director Stephen Mather, Dr. Jesse W. Fewkes, an unidentified laborer.

National Park Service. Fewkes was 58 years old when he arrived in the park, a seasoned Southwesterner, having done ethnographic research at Zuni and Hopi, excavations in the Hopi area and stabilization of Casa Grande National Monument in Arizona. He worked in the park off and on until 1922, when he was 72 years old. He died in 1930 at age 80.

Fewkes instituted such techniques as using native materials in his repairs, controlling runoff above a cliff dwelling by diverting water, capping walls exposed to rain or runoff with concrete, and building a shelter over a dirt-walled pithouse. Balcony House was the only site during this early period that Fewkes did not excavate and stabilize. Nusbaum did the early work there, working for Hewett of the Archaeological Institute of America, and using Fewkes' techniques and some of his crew. Neither man felt there was much left to learn from the ruins. They considered the cliff dwellings too damaged by looting to have significant undisturbed cultural deposits. Rather, both men considered architecture a setting for telling the story of the early village farmers, not something to be examined closely to determine how the villages grew, how the rooms functioned, or how the village layout changed through time.

Initial stabilization was done in conjunction with the excavation of sites. Soon after the formation of the park, Fewkes arrived ready to excavate and make repairs. His first choice was Spruce Tree House, which he repaired in May and June of 1908. His objective was entirely different from the Wetherills', and others' who did just about anything necessary to collect objects for museums and private collections, including ripping through floors, walls and roofs. J.W. Fewkes set out his stabilization philosophy in his first report.

> Archaeological experts may differ in their judgments regarding the extent of work necessary to repair a ruin as much mutilated as Spruce Tree House. It is difficult to determine a strict line of demarcation between repair and restoration work. The author has sought to avoid any restoration which would involve him in any theoretical questions even when he had good reasons to adopt an obvious interpretation. He has endeavored to preserve the picturesque character of the walls when possible and has not attempted to foist on the observer any theory of construction that was not clearly evident.

This was his "educational ideal for visitors." Fewkes also wanted his work to set a standard for stabilization, "an object lesson for archaeological students, showing by this means how ruins should be excavated and repaired." He wanted an end to sacrificing architectural data in the name of collecting artifacts for museums. He hoped that his work at Spruce Tree House, along with his earlier work at Casa Grande in Arizona, would convince archaeologists to take greater care in the treatment of ruins they excavated in the Southwest.

> Our responsibility in this work is very great, for we are dealing with precious data, which belongs to posterity as well as to the present generation. The author believes he has no right to tear down walls and despoil prehistoric cemeteries for any other purpose than the advancement of knowledge.

Much of Fewkes' original stabilization of Spruce Tree House is still intact almost 100 years later. Unfortunately, he felt the site was so disturbed that there was little chance for a great museum collection or that careful excavation would be productive. So he wrote frustratingly little about what he found, where he found it, and what modifications he made to the ruin.

The next year Fewkes tackled Cliff Palace, a 150-plus-room structure. This 1909 project took Fewkes and his crew three and a half months, mid-May to early August, and in 1911 he published a short report on this work. He repaired the fallen corner of the painted "tower" and filled in numerous holes that had been punched through the massive walls along the front of the site. Portland cement was used for the first time in the park, capping walls to deflect damaging alcove runoff.

"PORTLAND CEMENT WAS USED FOR THE FIRST TIME IN THE PARK, CAPPING WALLS TO DEFLECT DAMAGING ALCOVE RUNOFF."

The following year the Colorado Cliff Dwellings Association sponsored the excavation and repair of Balcony House. They contracted with Hewett, of the Archaeological Institute of America (the present School of American Research) in Santa Fe, who selected his protégé Jesse Nusbaum to do the work. Excavation and repair of the site took four weeks in October and November 1910. With a spring in the back of the alcove and the post-abandonment collapse of a portion of the roof, the site was in serious need of stabilization. To preserve as much of the upper walls as possible while replacing footer stones and pulling walls back to vertical, Nusbaum used angle iron, turnbuckles, and iron rods. In the ensuing years, no report was published on this work.

The next period of excavation/stabilization began in 1915, when Fewkes returned and did the first excavation of a mesa top site, Sun Temple. He also excavated a cliff dwelling, Oak Tree House, in what came to be named Fewkes Canyon, a drainage off Cliff Canyon. Sun Temple turned out to be a unique structure – not a habitation site at all – and Fewkes' romantic vision of prehistoric life on the mesa seems to

Dr. Jesse W. Fewkes at Far View Excavation in 1916.

have shaded his view of the structure. This isn't the only structure Fewkes named for postulated ceremonies of the past. Fire Temple, excavated in 1920, is also burdened with such a name. Most archaeologists still believe that both Sun Temple and Fire Temple are special sites, possibly ceremonial. But there is no evidence that Sun Temple was a temple or had anything to do with a special sun ceremony nor is there any evidence that Fire Temple had anything to do with a fire ceremony. Sun Temple is a mesa top site and, once dirt was removed from around the walls during excavation, its walls had no protection from rain. Fewkes realized the exposure would lead to immediate collapse of the walls unless something was done. So he returned to an approach he used on walls exposed to precipitation at Cliff Palace. He capped them with concrete – portland cement mixed with sand and some fairly large aggregate. That same year, 1915, Fewkes also inaugurated a park service tradition, the evening campfire program.

In 1916 Fewkes excavated the first mesa top habitation site, Far View House. Many archaeologists today would classify this site as a Chacoan outlier. Unfortunately Fewkes' method of rapid excavation and only cursory documentation makes interpretation difficult. Both Sun Temple and Far View House were built of massive walls. Again, to make the walls of Far View House impenetrable to rain, he capped them with concrete. At Sun Temple, Far View House and Cliff Palace, these caps have subsequently been replaced with stones set in a concrete mortar or with a colored concrete cap.

In 1917 Virginia McClurg and the Cliff Dwellings Association put on a

Colorado Historical Society

Virginia McClurg's "Marriage of the Dawn and Moon" performed in 1917 in Spruce Tree House, lasted one performance.

PAGEANTRY: GOOD OR BAD

The use of Spruce Tree House, in particular, for pageants, ballets, opera, Indian dances, and luminaria displays continues to the present time, and always raises the question of appropriateness. Where does Fewkes' educational ideal start sliding into recreation and a simple love of pageantry for its own sake? It is a continuing issue for park managers.

pageant set in Spruce Tree House. It was the first of a series of pageants using Spruce Tree House as a backdrop. In 1922 Nusbaum's wife staged a pageant and in 1931 Superintendent C. Marshall Finnan had a third kiva in Spruce Tree House roofed so his wife could hold a pageant.

In 1919 Fewkes returned to excavate and stabilize the cliff dwelling of Square Tower House, and Earth Lodge A (a pithouse) and a small pueblo on the mesa top near Square Tower. Fewkes built the park's first shelter over Earth Lodge A, beginning a long history of problems with shelters that includes a few successes and many failures. This pithouse was the first mesa top Basketmaker structure excavated in the park. Both it and the small pueblo have been backfilled and are not visible to the public.

Fewkes returned to the park for three more seasons of fieldwork. In 1920 he excavated and stabilized the Fewkes Canyon sites of Fire Temple and New Fire House. He also excavated and stabilized the mesa top site of Cedar Tree Tower, which consists of just a kiva and tower. He spent the season of 1921 excavating Painted Kiva House, named for the decorated plaster in one of the kivas. Then in 1922 Fewkes spent a busy season excavating in the Far View area: Pipe Shrine House, One Clan House, Far View Tower, and Megalithic House.

By 1922, 15 of the 16 sites excavated and stabilized by Fewkes were open to the public, along with Balcony House. Fewkes' great contribution was not only putting these fabulous ruins on exhibit, but also establishing standards in ruins stabilization that are followed to this day. Unfortunately he, like many who were to follow, found it difficult to adhere to the standards he established: to stabilize but not rebuild, to use original materials in the repairs, and to pass on the important knowledge he learned during excavation to future generations through a detailed published report.

Excavated mesa top sites with subsurface kivas and single wall construction, and without the protection of a shelter, are a big challenge for preservation. The walls will collapse once the mortar erodes out of wall joints, which happens with the first rain or snow storm. As early as Fewkes' time, to keep the walls standing, mortar joints in these walls were filled with concrete mortar, radi-

PUBLIC ACCESS

The Fewkes Canyon cliff dwellings were open to the public until the 1930s, when they were closed because of access problems. With increasing visitation in the park, the trail could not accommodate large numbers of people. Now these sites can be seen from an overlook on the Mesa Top Loop Road. Of the Far View area sites, all but One Clan House are still on exhibit to the public. Square Tower House was open to the public until the 1950s when lack of parking forced its closure. It can be seen from an overlook on the Mesa Top Loop Road and is, in fact, one of the most photographed cliff dwellings in the park.

cally modifying the walls' appearance. The cliff dwellings' protected locations have made that tactic unnecessary and preserved both the aesthetic appeal and the integrity of the structures. Of the mesa top sites exposed during excavation, many of the massive walls of Sun Temple and Far View House are original with only replacement mortar on the surface of joints and with the walls capped. But in the narrow single-course walls of Pipe Shrine House, Coyote Village, and parts of Far View House, only the stones of the walls are original. Earthen bedding mortar has long since been replaced with a concrete mortar and in many cases, many times over.

The Years of Neglect, 1922-1934

The 12 years following Fewkes' 1922 departure were a time of park infrastructure construction: housing, museum, offices, and roads. With the excavated and stabilized cliff dwellings and mesa top sites open to the public in the summer when the park was open, attention turned to the need to provide for people's comfort and safety while visiting the park. There was a concern for developing problems in the excavated sites — wet and sagging walls, and dust — but no funding or staff to address them.

Nonetheless, a very important event for the park occurred in 1921, just before Fewkes' last season in the park. Jesse Nusbaum was named superintendent. He first came to the park in 1907 as part of a survey crew for Hewett. He returned in 1908, and then in 1910 was assigned the project of excavating and stabilizing Balcony House. During these years his interest in photography and archaeology resulted in some of the most important historic documents we have of the cliff dwellings — a vast collection of

Step House excavation in 1926.
From left to right: Jim Corn, Sam Ahkeah, Deric Nusbaum, Marshall Finnan,
Jim Nair, Clint Scharf and Jesse Nusbaum. Sam Ahkeah became a good friend of Jesse
Nusbaum. Later in life he was a chairman of the Navajo Tribe, in the late '40s and early '50s.

photographs now in the photo archives of the Museum of New Mexico. Now he was returning as superintendent and it was Nusbaum, even more than Fewkes who would define what came to be thought of as Mesa Verde National Park. As a manager Nusbaum continued his interest in archaeology but the real emphasis during all of his years in the park was development of the park for the public.

Between his Balcony House work and his return to Mesa Verde, Nusbaum had excavated a Basketmaker site (Dupont Cave) in Utah, which led to a continuing interest in this early period of Pueblo prehistory. During the '20s the new superintendent spent winters with a field crew looking for artifacts for his new museum. This drive for artifacts led to the exploration of many cliff dwellings on Wetherill Mesa and Moccasin Mesa – a return to the late 19th century desire for "stuff" for museums. As part of this project and to further his interest in the early occupation of alcoves, Nusbaum excavated in Step House in 1926, a site which Nordenskiöld had already studied finding what he believed to be early deposits. Nusbaum excavated the pithouses in the lowest portion of the alcove.

It was during the Nusbaum years that the use of Navajo laborers on park crews was established. He was frustrated that "Mancos boys" would leave when they found better jobs in town. Working with small appropriations, Nusbaum was able to pay Navajos less than the Mancos workers, and had the added benefit that Navajos were far enough from home that he had a stable work force once they were in the park. He even built housing specifically for them – the only ethnic housing in the National Park Service.

In a few areas, Nusbaum's judgement can certainly be questioned. Stone from Spruce Tree House was used in the construction of the superintendent's residence and he excavated sites that are on Ute land, outside the boundary of the park.

NUSBAUM'S DOCUMENTATION

Nusbaum's excavations are poorly documented. He found the work frustrating because the sites had been disturbed by early explorers. They are frustrating as well for recent archaeologists who find it impossible to determine where Nusbaum excavated. The desire for museum quality objects led to the destruction of many deposits that surely would have increased our knowledge of the life of the builders and occupants of the cliff dwellings.

The Lancaster Years, 1934-1964: The Years of Major Projects

Finally after years of neglect to the cliff dwellings and other ruins, the New Deal came to the rescue. The park benefited greatly from the special programs developed in Washington D.C. to stimulate the economy and create jobs during the Great Depression. In 1933 New Deal programs and funds became available for repairs and, for the first time, park staff became involved with the repair and excavation of ruins. Previously, people were hired under contract to do the excavation and stabilization. By the early 1930s, almost all of the major cliff dwellings needed attention. Practically as soon as Nusbaum left Balcony House in 1910, the superintendent wrote memos about problems with water in the kivas. The spring in Cliff Palace was causing problems and the level of dust in the cliff dwellings was mentioned as a constant irritant to visitors.

In early 1934 archaeologist Earl Morris, known for his work at Aztec Ruins in New Mexico, was put in charge of the Works Progress Administration projects in Mesa Verde. Morris took a temporary leave of absence from the Carnegie Institution and returned to his position at that institution in less than a year. He was hired to develop a ruins "stabilization and repair" program, but continued to be busy in New Mexico and made only short visits to Mesa Verde.

James A. (Al) Lancaster was hired to assist in this program and then took over as director in late 1934. His illustrious career with the excavation and stabilization program of Mesa Verde National Park would extend three

Camp of a repair crew at Mug House in 1935.
From left to right: Willie Ahkeah, Al Lancaster, Roy Dobbins, John Charlie,
Con Jean Howe and H. Boyland.

decades, to 1964. Lancaster always described himself as a failed bean farmer from Pleasant View – a small village in the Montezuma Valley north of Cortez. His first excavations were in 1928 in his own backyard when the Chicago Field Museum excavated Lowry Ruins. He was always very aware of his lack of formal education, but the archaeologist that he spent a lifetime assisting deferred to his wealth of practical knowledge when in the field. In 1931-33 he worked in Southwest Utah for J.O. Brew, of the Peabody Museum. After he began his career in Mesa Verde in 1934-35, he worked in the Hopi area, again for J.O. Brew of the Peabody Museum. In 1939 he returned to the park, serving as the field man for ruins and working as much on excavation as stabilization. But his position was not always funded, so from 1944 to 1947 he was at Aztec and then Chaco as a park ranger and archaeological aide. Finally, in 1947 he was hired full time at Mesa Verde as an archaeological aide. Even after his mandatory retirement in 1964, he continued work in Mesa Verde as an employee of the University of Colorado.

By the 1930s all of the sites excavated by Fewkes, as well as the one excavated by Nusbaum, were in need of at least some attention. Several had major problems. The years of little or no maintenance convinced park managers that "ruins" needed attention if they were to retain their appearance, and that maintenance to the sites needed to last since no one knew when the next funding would be available. Lancaster came to the rescue of these rapidly deteriorating ruins, using mortars with higher clay content than the original earthen mortars, but also using portland cement as both an additive to, and a replacement for, earthen mortar. Fewkes had used portland cement to cap walls exposed to rain or alcove runoff. Lancaster expanded its use on both the cliff dwellings and the mesa top sites, not only capping walls, but also setting deteriorating basal stones with it. Unstable bedrock boulders were held in place by concrete, and even trails were hardened with concrete.

JAMES A. LANCASTER

When Al Lancaster retired from the park service, he was recognized with the highest award in the National Park Service, a Distinguished Service Award. This was the person whose shoes I was supposed to fill – a rather daunting task. I met him several times and interviewed him once. His interest and regard for the archaeological resources was evident until his death in Cortez in 1992 at the age of 98.

Because of the obvious problems associated with the use of portland cement – both its aesthetics and its deleterious effect on original fabric – it is easy to be critical of this choice of material. But many walls now stand, even in a deteriorated state, because portland cement was used; without it the walls would have fallen. Through the years, the park service simply has not provided enough maintenance funding to allow for the use of native materials. It has been an ongoing challenge to stabilization through Mesa Verde's first century: What level of funding is appropriate? What materials are appropriate?

Lancaster hired a crew that included Anglo craftsmen, carpenters primarily, and Navajo laborers, whom he trained as stonemasons, a mixture of skills and cultures that would be maintained on the park stabilization crew for years to come. Cliff Palace was the first to receive help. In 1934 the cracked boulder under Speaker Chief's House was stabilized with concrete and rebar. Concrete was placed behind a wall of facing stones in an effort to stabilize the boulder, which had cracked at some time in the past, undoubtedly due to moisture from the spring in the back of the site. Another project in Cliff Palace was the reconstruction of a corner of the four-story painted "tower." This area that had been rebuilt by Fewkes was again in need of rebuilding.

At Balcony House the kivas had to be rebuilt because of moisture problems. A trench was constructed in the back of the alcove that captured the water from the spring, collecting it in a small reservoir and then piped it around the kivas to the front of the ledge.

In this same period – 1933 and 1934 – Spruce Tree House, Cliff

Cliff Palace in 1934. The crew here was rebuilding a corner of the painted "tower." Al Lancaster is second from left.

Palace, and Far View House were to be documented with detailed maps and photographs. Every wall was to be photographed, with all physical characteristics carefully delineated. Detailed plan view maps were made of every wall and room, and each site as a whole. In the future, the detailed information "may be used as authentic source for material in connection with their repair and preservation." Archaeologist Earl Morris was a supporter of documentation prior to repairs or reconstruction and felt that the unprecedented level of documentation of original fabric and stabilization repairs at Mesa Verde – although time-consuming and therefore expensive – should continue so that there would be no question as to what was old and what was new. But there was a "never-ending struggle between the ideal and the expedient." Then, after two years, funding disappeared so the mapping and photographic project was never completed and the desire for in-depth documentation went largely unfulfilled. Before and after photos were compiled, however, as well as brief descriptions of the repairs.

When I arrived in the park, notebooks containing the photographs taken during these projects were available and extensively used for determining stabilization histories of various site walls. The site maps had been misplaced and were not available until recently when they were "found" and used as base maps for detailed mapping projects in Spruce Tree House and Cliff Palace.

Fewkes' and Nusbaum's work established the physical context for much of the park's interpretation on Chapin Mesa. The only later additions were the excavation of early mesa top Pueblo villages on what became the Chapin Mesa Loop Road, a seventh century pithouse to replace the collapsed Earth Lodge A Fewkes had excavated, and then four sites dating from 700 to 1200. Right before World War II, in the last years of Depression era projects, Fewkes' Earth Lodge A was damaged when the shelter collapsed. This pithouse was then backfilled and another excavated - Pithouse B that is now on exhibit as the first stop along the Chapin Mesa Loop Road.

At about this time interest grew in having an exhibit of archaeological sites that would display the sequence of Pueblo village development through time, including an early pithouse and villages dating to 700, 900, and so on. The mesa top interpretive loop was developed after the war and remains a unique "drive through time." It shows how Pueblo architecture changed, with the early shallow pithouse evolving into deeper and deeper pithouses and finally the very formalized cliff dwelling kivas; and with the crude storage rooms built near pithouses evolving into more substantial storage rooms and jacal villages and ending with stone-walled villages. Unfortunately many of the sites picked for exhibition turned out to have complex histories with a village of one period built over a village of a later period. Consequently, understanding takes a little effort. The "tour" ends at an overlook with a spectacular view of 12 cliff dwellings in Fewkes and Cliff canyons, including Cliff Palace.

While work was being done on interpretive exhibits, the park staff was also involved in a survey of the park's archaeological resources. This had started in the 1940s and continued off and on as staff and time allowed. The survey was concentrated on Chapin Mesa. In the 1950s, excavation was again undertaken and this time with the introduction of a field school from the University of Colorado. They excavated sites in the Far View area that were then stabilized and covered with low temporary shelters. The subsurface features of these sites were backfilled in the 1980s when it was finally decided that they would not be put on exhibit.

By the 1950s congestion led to the decision to move several support facilities off Chapin Mesa and to interpret sites elsewhere in the park, specifically Wetherill Mesa. After Chapin Mesa, Wetherill Mesa contains the largest concentration of cliff dwellings. So the primary objective was to replicate on Wetherill Mesa what was available on Chapin Mesa. The other goal was research. Many of the sites on Chapin Mesa were poorly understood due to the lack of data acquired during their excavation and repair. With support from both the park service and the National Geographic Society, there was funding to do survey, excavation, stabilization and related research. The objective was to better understand the society that lived on the Mesa Verde from 600 to 1300 by intensively studying this one area of the park. During the Wetherill Mesa Project (1958-65), the cliff dwellings of Long House, Step House, and Mug House were excavated and stabilized, and the mesa top community of Badger House was excavated, then protected by erection of temporary shelters over portions of these sites. The Wetherill Mesa Project turned out to be a rather typical National Park Service project. It got off to a great start but completion dragged on. The research component, in fact, had a pretty good track record. Excavation and stabilization were completed and most reports were eventually completed and published. Some took awhile with Two Raven House published in 1988 and Step House still awaiting publication. The temporary shelters collapsed before permanent ones were built. Initially only Long House was open to the public. Now Long House, Step House, and Badger House Community are open from Memorial Day to Labor Day. Mug House is only open for special tours at the discretion of the superintendent.

Staff of the Wetherill Mesa Project photographed above Long House, 1960. 1. Lancaster, 2. Hannah, 3. Fairer, 4. Tapahonso, 5. Rienau, 6. Hayes, 7. Pond, 8. King, 9. Williams, 10. Decker, 11. Cattanach, 12. Wade, 13. Lewis, 14. Nelson, 15. J. Begay, 16. Brew, 17. Mrs. Rienau, 18. Rohn, 19. Lalander, 20. Loy, 21. Nichols, 22. Melbye, 23. Joe, 24. Bluehorse, 25. Ruckel, 26. Ellis, 27. Haury, 28. R. Begay, 29. Lee, 30. Sanchez, 31. Yeoman, 32. Frank, 33. Fitzgerald, 34. Wood.

At the same time as the Wetherill Project was in full gear, projects financed in part by Mission 66 funds were being built. The campground on Chapin Mesa was reworked into a picnic area and a new campground was built in Morefield Canyon. A visitor center was built at the north end of Chapin Mesa, in the Far View area. The concessions buildings (a lodge, gas station, and cabins) near the museum were torn down and a new complex of buildings was constructed by the concessionaire near the new Visitor Center. In fact the park as we see it today was in place by the 1960s – not everything was open but the facilities were built.

It was in these same years, 1950s and early 1960s, that some big stabilization projects were undertaken. In particular a tunnel was excavated under Cliff Palace to address a continuing water problem and pins were used to stabilize the alcove above Spruce Tree House.

The Decker-Crawford Years, 1964-1986: Finally a Permanent Crew

Al Decker, who had been hired as a carpenter on the Wetherill Mesa Project, supervised the crew for 16 years after Al Lancaster retired. After

Decker, Ron Crawford supervised the crew. Crawford had worked for Al Decker and also had a strong crafts background. He had been, and would return to, teaching carpentry to high school students. Many of the crew members during the Decker-Crawford years were originally hired by Lancaster. Lancaster's traditions were maintained and valued by the crew. One big improvement during this period was the change from a stabilization crew that worked from project to project, crisis to crisis, to a permanent crew which could finally establish and maintain a cycle of monitoring and repairing.

It was also during this period that the park service, as an institution, began to realize that a more scientific approach to stabilization might be of benefit. A major study of mud mortar additives was made at Chaco and the problems with portland cement began to appear and be discussed. The life of a mud mortar clearly still had to be extended in order for walls to remain standing. Park budgets could not support enough employees to constantly re-point walls with unamended earthen mortars. Yet mortars that were harder than the surrounding stones accelerated the stones' deterioration by forcing moisture through them. At Mesa Verde experiments with such earthen mortar additives as calcium aluminate and acrylic polymers were initiated and by the time I came to the park, an acrylic polymer was the standard additive in Mesa Verde and in most parks in the Southwest where mud mortars had been used in the original construction.

Right after the Wetherill Mesa Archaeological Project closed, another research project began with an agreement between the NPS and the University of Colorado, in 1965-77. Funds were supplied by both institutions and by the National Science Foundation. Many of the current professionals in the field of southwestern archaeology got their start during this project, much of it involving salvage archaeology – excavating sites before they were destroyed for development of park facilities, including campgrounds and roads. Also, Coyote Village in the Far View area was excavated in 1968-69 and the rest of the park was surveyed (Chapin and Wetherill mesas had been surveyed earlier). Coyote Village was to round out the interpretive scheme for the Far View area. In fact what was thought to be a Pueblo III village turned out to be a site which also had Pueblo I and II occupations with evidence of much rebuilding.

The Fiero Years, 1986-2002: Incremental Change

I was completely overwhelmed by my new job in 1986. The standard stabilization methods used by federal agencies were under fire. The work load included hundreds of cliff dwellings, thousands of mesa top sites, the repair of more than 20 historic stone buildings, plus the stabilization of ruins in Hovenweep National Monument. At the same time, funding and crew size was on a downward trend.

Stabilization crew at Far View Ruin site 808, in 1964.
Back row from left: Jim Begay, George King, Lewis Joe, James Frank, Jim Frank
Front row from left: Al Decker, Al Lancaster, Raymond Begay and Les Golf.

A lot of time was spent during those early years thinking about stabilization needs, packaging them as projects, determining their cost and then selling the projects to park managers. This experience led to a formalized preservation plan which defined the goals of stabilization. It was apparent that a maintenance cycle could only be established and followed with reliable funding. I also applied for grants to handle backcountry stabilization and other special projects such as stabilization work on the historic buildings and tree ring dating.

After gaining some competence with standard stabilization problems and projects – cleaning, weeding, assessing condition, re-pointing, all with appropriate documentation – I branched out into other areas.

I focused first on Balcony House; I wanted to do research and picked a cliff dwelling that was very poorly documented. My research included examining the original excavation documents as well as the walls and datable wood of the site. The sampling of datable wood was so successful that this project was expanded to include sampling wood in other cliff dwellings.

Then a crisis with a deteriorating sandstone boulder under a two-story tower at Hovenweep National Monument led to research into techniques for preserving sandstone with chemical additives. The continuing deterioration of earthen plasters on cliff dwelling walls led to a project to deter-

Stabilization crew in North Plaza, Balcony House, in 1995.
From left: Gene Trujillo, Willie Begay, Kee Charley John, Kathy Fiero and Raymond Begay.

mine their physical and chemical composition. This program also included developing and testing various approaches to preserving these plasters. There was also an expansion into the documentation of rock art after a wildland fire damaged one of only two large rock art panels in the park.

All of these projects involved, to varying degrees, both the stabilization staff and outside consultants and contractors. The one completely in-house project was cataloging all previously uncataloged stabilization photographs. Done over a period of many years, it was finally completed just before I left Mesa Verde.

All of this occurred in an atmosphere of constantly changing budgets and the resultant changes in crew size. Mesa Verde wasn't the only park with huge preservation problems and declining funding. Three Southwest r egion parks pressed their needs to regional and national levels. The result was the Vanishing Treasures initiative which focused on increasing funding, improving training, and adding permanent positions to park stabilization programs. The Mesa Verde stabilization program greatly benefited from this initiative with training, an increase in permanent positions and funding for special projects. As staffing and funding improved, projects that were identified in the preservation plan were implemented. They included the documentation, assessment of condition, and stabilization of back-country cliff dwellings; creation and maintenance of an electronic site database; in-depth documentation of Oak Tree House, Cliff Palace, and Spruce Tree House; and the editing and publishing of my Balcony House report.

During my years in Mesa Verde, there was a definite reduction in the one-time, major construction projects. Many of those earlier projects had been very successful, such as the tunnel at Cliff Palace, the water diversion at Balcony House and the stabilization of the "arch" above Spruce Tree House. It wasn't that I was against such large projects. The change in

---

"THE VARIED PROJECTS WITH WHICH I WAS INVOLVED, AND THE RESULTANT SUCCESSES AND FAILURES, LED TO MY OBSESSION WITH CLIFF DWELLINGS."

---

emphasis related to my background as an archaeologist. Instead of carpentry and construction, my approach was to do lots of testing with small-scale interventions. Rather than big projects, we focused on numerous small ones – multi-year projects, tree ring research, stone stabilization, plaster preservation, rock art documentation and Balcony House research – done by either the stabilization crew or appropriate professionals hired specifically for the project. The varied projects with which I was involved, and the resultant successes and failures, led to my obsession with cliff dwellings.

4

WORKING ON THE MESA:
WHAT A STABILIZATION CREW DOES

"The Mesa Verde is unique in its educational importance. It is destined ultimately to be a Mecca for all students of the prehistory of the Southwest and an object lesson to all visitors who wish to see the best preserved buildings of pre-Columbian times in our country. It is self-evident that the excavation and repair of all the ruins in this park can not be accomplished in a few years, even were it desirable to attempt it; the work means many years of arduous devotion, intelligently directed, and a large sum of money. It is desirable to open up these precious remains of antiquity care-fully, following a definite plan, availing ourselves of methods acquired by experience. The work should be done with care, and it will be an addition-al attraction if visitors can see how the work is done."

J. Walter Fewkes
Publication on the excavation of Sun Temple, 1917

MY WORK IN RUINS

I n 1986, as the new supervisor of stabilization at Mesa Verde National Park, I was put in charge of a very experienced, primarily Navajo crew of men. That first year I was a little nervous around them. They knew so much more than I did. As an archaeologist, I was trained to take notes, so they did things and I took notes on exactly what they did and where. Over the winter, while the crew was off, I decided that had to change. I had to know why they did what they did. I had to understand the process, the goals and objectives. So for the next several years, I worked with the stabilization crew every day, all day – hoeing weeds, re-pointing walls, sweeping rooms, and cleaning drainage ditches. That is really when my educa-tion in preservation began and when I first developed a plan for how I would approach the varied problems the crew had to address.

The first question was where to concentrate efforts among Mesa Verde's cliff dwellings, mesa top and canyon bottom pithouses and masonry vil-lages, check dams and farm terraces, towers and ceremonial rooms. Needless to say, it is the experienced stabilization crew that gave the pro-gram continuity and was responsible for its success all through my years there. My most important accomplishments are a much better understand-ing of the construction history of Balcony House; an approach to the preservation of plasters on the walls of many cliff dwellings; the establish-ment of a project to record the pictographs and petroglyphs in the park; the implementation of a project to date the wood in rooms and features of the larger cliff dwellings; and a preservation plan for Square Tower and the boulder on which it is built in Hovenweep National Monument.

Another of my priorities was to develop a history of stabilization activi-ties. Quite a bit of preservation work had been done in the park prior to my arrival, over a long enough period that no one on the crew could remember everything that had happened. There were photographs of many of the specific walls and features the stabilization crew had modified through the years, but not all. And many of the photographs were not cataloged by site, room, feature, or date. Jesse Fewkes, who had stabilized all but one of the major cliff dwellings on Chapin Mesa, is notorious for his scanty notes and very general reports. Jesse Nusbaum, who stabilized Balcony House, never published a report. Luckily the major cliff dwellings on Wetherill Mesa were excavated in the early 1960s when the standards for documentation were better; reports had been written and in most cases published, and the photographs were cataloged. So the problem was concentrated on the Chapin Mesa sites.

For those sites, it was impossible in many cases to tell whether loss was of recent stabilization material or original Pueblo material, which are treated differently. Original material is of great importance and any loss reduces the authenticity of the site. If deterioration is of known stabilization material, then the loss isn't so serious, but knowing the date of the repair helps to gauge its effectiveness. So I began by examining park documents and cataloging the backlog of stabilization photographs. The photo backlog was so huge that this project was only completed a few years before I left the park; now of course all these photos need to be digitized. The final need was for a wall-by-wall examination of the sites, a process that is still being completed for many of the cliff dwellings.

THE JOB

I divided the cliff dwellings and other archaeological sites we stabilized into three categories in terms of public access: front-country sites (which are excavated, stabilized, and entered by the public); mid-country sites (which are excavated, stabilized, and with one exception visible to the public but not entered by them); and backcountry sites, not seen (with three exceptions that are visible from overlooks) or entered by the public and not excavated.

The front-country sites not only had to be stable and safe for preservation reasons, but also safe for the public in those areas they were allowed to enter. Our work there focused on walkways, weeds and walls. Mid-country sites needed to be stable and safe for the resource but also had to look good, so stabilization focused on weeds and walls. The backcountry sites had to be stable and safe for the resource, so stabilization concentrated on walls.

The cliff dwellings were constructed exclusively of local materials. The wood is primarily juniper and pinyon, with some fir. The stone is Cliff House sandstone. The mortar is local dirt mixed with water. Windblown reddish soil which covers the mesa was used for mortar in the mesa top sites. In the cliff dwellings, the more tan alluvial soils around the alcoves were used for mortar. Cliff dwelling walls are built in one of three ways:

■ Wet-laid, with stones set in a mud mortar (the standard technique in all the cliff dwellings)

■ Dry-laid mudded, with the stones set one on top of the other and then mudded (not common in the cliff dwellings)

■ Dry-laid, with stones set without mortar (very uncommon in the cliff

CROSS-SECTION OF WALLS

MORTAR IN WALL

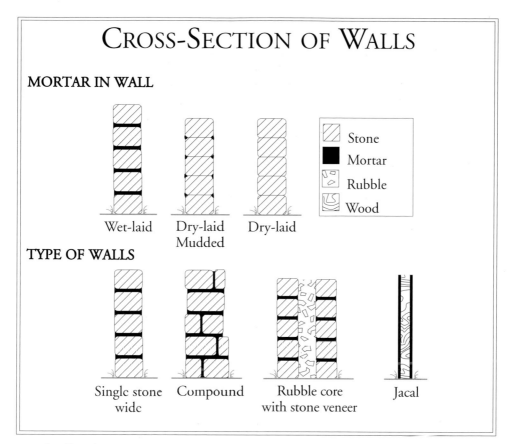

Stone
Mortar
Rubble
Wood

Wet-laid   Dry-laid   Dry-laid
             Mudded

TYPE OF WALLS

Single stone   Compound   Rubble core   Jacal
wide   with stone veneer

dwellings).

Most room walls are a single stone or a stone and a half wide. In walls that are a single stone wide, typically both faces of the stone are shaped at least to some extent. In compound, stone-and-a-half-wide walls, the exposed faces of exterior wall stones are shaped and the uneven interior surface smoothed out with the addition of small stones and lots of mortar. A few walls were built with a stone veneer and a rubble core and even fewer are jacal. Builders chipped and pecked sandstone to create rectangular blocks that look something like a loaf of bread. This shaping could be done very carefully or left fairly crude. Some stones were left unshaped but most have some shaping on at least one and sometimes all surfaces. Almost all wall stones were laid horizontally but there are examples of upright stones being used to create room walls. Also, door jambs were sometimes created by setting a stone upright.

In Mesa Verde a standard finishing technique was inserting small stones, or less often broken pottery or dried corn cobs, into mortar joints. In order to recreate the original appearance, the stabilization crew added these chinking stones, chinkers for short, when stabilization required replacement of missing mortar. The purpose of these stones has been debated.

SITES AND PUBLIC ACCESS

FRONT-COUNTRY CLIFF DWELLINGS
Chapin Mesa: Spruce Tree House, Cliff Palace, Balcony House
Wetherill Mesa: Long House, Step House

FRONT-COUNTRY MESA TOP SITES
Chapin Mesa: pithouses and early villages on Mesa Top Loop Road; Far View group (Far View House, Pipe Shrine House, Coyote Village, Far View Tower, Far View Reservoir, Megalithic House); Cedar Tree Tower, Farm Terraces, Sun Temple
Wetherill Mesa: Badger House Community

MID-COUNTRY CLIFF DWELLINGS*
Chapin Mesa: Square Tower House, Oak Tree House, Fire Temple, New Fire House
Wetherill Mesa: Mug House#

BACKCOUNTRY CLIFF DWELLINGS: 600-PLUS SITES
Chapin Mesa: Sunset House+
Wetherill Mesa: Kodak House+, Nordenskiöld 16+

BACKCOUNTRY MESA TOP SITES: 4,600-PLUS SITES

* excavated and stabilized but not open to the general public; Chapin Mesa sites are visible from Mesa Top Loop Road
# Open by special request to the park superintendent
+ visible from overlooks

Gustaf Nordenskiöld, an early researcher, thought they added stability to the wall. Jesse Fewkes, who was responsible for more excavations within the park than any other archaeologist, thought they were for decoration and protection against the rapid loss of mortar. I think they had multiple purposes: to level stones during construction, to press mortar firmly into the joint after setting a stone, for decoration, for better adherence of plaster, and for tradition – just the right way to finish a joint.

At Mesa Verde the mortar is typically what is called "extruded smoothed," in which the joint was filled with mortar extending slightly past the wall plane, and then hand-smoothed. Then chinking stones were added. Many walls were then covered at least in part with one to numerous coats of a thin earthen plaster. Often, numerous contiguous walls were plastered, sometimes entire rooms. In some cases only the lower walls of rooms were plastered, creating a dado. Many, if not most, of the walls encircling some courtyards were plastered. Rooms can be alone or as part of a cluster of rooms. They can receive support from the alcove or be freestanding. They can be completely above ground, partially below grade or completely subterranean, such as the walls of many kivas.

Visitors often ask how many rooms are in a particular cliff dwelling, presuming they were living space, as we use rooms today, and all were used at the same time. In actuality, cliff dwelling rooms served several purposes. Some were for domestic purposes such as sleeping and eating. Others were for storage, and some may have had multiple purposes or their use may have changed through time, such as a sleeping room reused for storage. Still other rooms may have been abandoned at the same time others were being built.

The function of a room is not always easy to determine.

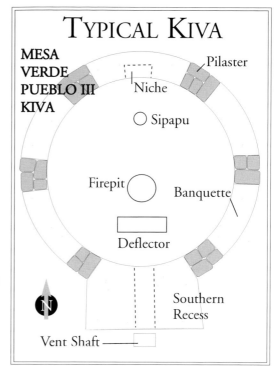

TYPICAL KIVA

MESA VERDE PUEBLO III KIVA

Pilaster

Niche

Sipapu

Firepit

Banquette

Deflector

N

Southern Recess

Vent Shaft

Very small rooms with low walls were probably for storage. Big rooms with hearths were probably for sleeping and eating. But there are also fairly large rooms with no hearth, and very small rooms with sooted walls. Round rooms classified as towers are a problem. Typically they have no floor features. Round rooms called kivas are considered ceremonial because of their numerous special features such as deflector, sipapu, wall niches, and vent shaft. But with the heaviest sooting and most well-used hearths in a cliff dwelling in kivas, they also seem to have been used for sleeping and eating. The function of rooms with a series of grinding stones set in bins, termed mealing bins, is fairly obvious: food preparation.

Rooms contain such features as hearths, sticks set in joint mortar used as wall pegs, small rectangular openings for ventilation, wall loops, and of course, doorways. Doorways vary in type: Some are small and rectangular; others are larger and T-shaped. Almost all doorways are raised, with the sill above the level of the floor. The smaller rectangular doorways were covered from the outside with a slab of stone. Those doorways include mud lines along the door jambs and a stick parallel to and right below the lintel which acted as the doorstop. The stone rested against this stick. In T-shaped doorways with sticks right below the lintel, the sticks may have been used to suspend a woven mat. T-shaped doorways are associated with bigger rooms containing hearths, undoubtedly living rooms. These rooms face the courtyard. Storage rooms can also face the courtyard but some are accessed from living rooms.

The distance the doorsill was raised above the floor level varies dramatically. Some are low enough that one can easily step into the room, but others are so high that it is very awkward to enter the room. Why they were built that way is not known. Entry into some rooms is very difficult because the sill is so high.

The other type of room opening is the hatchway found in the roofs of kivas, and sometimes in the corner of roofs/floors between first- and second-story rooms. In a kiva, a ladder would have been placed between the hatchway and floor. In rooms, small stones set in the wall of the lower room or depressions in the wall were used to ascend/descend through the hatchway.

MESA TOP SITES

The mesa top sites, which vary in age from the 6th to the 13th century, are more of a challenge to stabilize than the cliff dwellings. The techniques for constructing walls and roofs varied through time and often these walls were more fragile, simply the earth walls of a pit, or mud applied to a weak framework of wood. The earliest structures are semi-subterranean pithouses. A fairly shallow, wide hole was dug in the ground and the walls were then plastered. The Pueblo builders used only earthen plasters. From the earliest periods on the mesa through the cliff dwelling period, the plasters often have a high calcium carbonate component due to the caliche in the soil used for plaster. It is white to cream-colored and was used to create a whitish earthen plaster. Iron oxide, also common on Mesa Verde, was added to create a deep red plaster.

Through time, the pithouses became deeper and finally evolved into the very stylized Mesa Verde Pueblo III kiva with its stone-lined walls. Early stone-lined storage cists evolved through time into above-ground walls of small diameter wood covered with mortar and later into stone-walled storage and habitation rooms. Stone is a relatively hard material, earth is not. So the more stone used in the construction of a room or feature, the easier the repair. The most difficult preservation problems at Mesa Verde include the rebuilding of collapsed earthen walls such as pithouse walls. In such cases a new wall has to be constructed, but the final product needs to look like the natural undisturbed soil, which is not at all easy.

During the final period of mesa top construction, the Pueblo III period, some buildings were constructed using shaped stone laid in mortar with compound and/or core and veneer walls, which have a dirt core and stone veneer on each face. Without the protection of an alcove, the roofs all collapsed well before the 20th century but some walls still stand. In most cases these walls have been exposed through excavation but there are examples in the park of standing walls that were never protected by wind-blown deposits or the natural collapse of the surrounding walls and roofs. In cases like this, the stone is relatively stable, certainly relative to the earthen mortar, which erodes out of the joints with every rain storm and can de-stabilize the wall.

Whether the function of the ruins is education or research, there are just a few causes of stabilization problems. But any one of them can play havoc with a site.

The major problem is water – from above as rainwater, from within as a spring in an alcove, or from below as rising damp. In cliff dwellings, water can flow over the lip of the alcove and land on walls and trash deposits. At Mesa Verde, Jesse Fewkes first approached this problem at Spruce Tree House by digging a ditch on the slickrock above the site to divert water away from the lip of the alcove. His approach has been implemented above almost every large cliff dwelling in the park's front-country and in some cases for backcountry sites. Once ditches and berms are in place, the con-

---

"INEVITABLY, THROUGH TIME THE MOISTURE AND SALTS LEAD TO DISINTEGRATION OF THE MORTAR AND STONES."

---

cern is to maintain them. In some cases scuppers have been used to carry the water well out in front of the site before it drops. These scuppers can be seen above Spruce Tree House and Kodak House. Another approach is to modify the alcove's dripline by placing a copper strip in the lip of the alcove roof, as can be seen over Square Tower House and Spruce Tree House.

While ditches and berms take work to build, implanting copper lips in sandstone high above a site is much harder and more dangerous. This was done in the 1930s-'50s from a platform suspended by rope over the lip of the alcove. More recently, a bead of silicone caulking has been applied to alcoves above cliff dwellings to modify driplines, an idea that came from Australia where the technique was used to modify driplines around rock art panels. To my knowledge, it was first used in the United States by a private contractor at Hovenweep and then I used the technique on numerous front- and backcountry sites in Mesa Verde. The technique is inexpensive, reversible, and has a very long life, but is dependent on stability of the sandstone. If a sandstone flake on which silicone has been placed pops off during a fire or for other reasons, of course the silicone is dislodged with it. The challenge of using silicone is that a person must work from a ladder to apply it, or in many cases where the alcove is high, work off ropes with harness.

On mesa top sites, the approach to rainwater problems has been to build shelters such as those on the Mesa Top Loop Road and in Badger House Community, or to cap walls such as seen at Far View House and

Sun Temple. Wall caps are typically made of a non-native material, some kind of cement or acrylic. Although they very often don't work well, they are still better than earthen mortar alone. The problem, of course, is that these structures were designed to have a roof and now do not. Metal pipes have been installed at the wall bases to move water from the interior to the exterior. In some cases after a heavy rain a sump pump is used to remove water from kivas, such as those in Coyote Village and Cedar Tree Tower.

Water can also be found within a site. In cliff dwellings it is quite common to have an active spring in the alcove, a much more difficult problem to deal with than water cascading over an alcove lip. Here we must constantly remember that we don't want to destroy a site to save it. When modifications to the site are too intrusive, we lose much of the original fabric (architectural materials) that we were trying to save. Balcony House is a real success story in moving spring water.

Rising damp is the hardest problem to deal with in cliff dwellings and open sites. Moisture in the sandstone comes up into the walls, making the stones moist and depositing salts on their surface. Inevitably, through time the moisture and salts lead to disintegration of the mortar and stones. Unfortunately there is not much that can be done about it. Kivas often suffer from rising damp because their walls are the lowest in the cliff dwellings. The problem is exacerbated by cycles of wet and dry conditions. Walls that stay wet or dry are much more stable. At areas of a site that are not visible to the public, the best approach is to cover these walls with fill. When this is done, it is the fill which is exposed and will deteriorate, not the kiva wall.

Archaeologists hate backfilling – who wants to cover what has just recently been exposed? It is time-consuming and hard work, but oh so necessary. There is no other way that excavated sites can be returned to as stable an environment as the one that was destroyed by excavation. Of course, if the excavated site is to be a display for the public, backfilling the viewed area is not possible. Nor is it the answer for walls that have never in the past been covered with fill. But for appropriate sites not on exhibit, careful backfilling saves original fabric and thousands of dollars in preservation costs.

Backfilling a kiva requires lots of dirt being lowered into the alcove, and it removes a resource from interpretation and visibility. A lot of backfilling has been done in the Southwest recently and I'm a big advocate. Walls are removed from the maintenance cycle, leaving more time for other walls and features.

After water, all other stabilization problems seem simple. Where plants hold moisture and obscure walls and wall features, weeds are cut. Although simple, it can take much effort and many days each season. Poison ivy caused me and a few other crew members fits, but on the whole, plants are the easy part of the program. Insects, in particular ground bees, are a concern at Step House and the early pithouse in Badger House Community.

Rodents are a major problem, in particular ground squirrels. I tried many things to control their digging: live traps to move them, moth balls to discourage them. Needless to say, what I learned is that they are much more persistent than I. Basically, nine times out of 10, they win.

Of lesser concern but still a problem are birds. Vultures raise their young in backcountry cliff dwellings, laying their eggs amongst fallen wall stones, and they roost in front of and sometimes on the walls of Spruce Tree House. Other birds like cliff dwellings for perching and housing. Swifts and swallows are always flying around Cliff Palace. A spotted owl was seen perched on a wall of that dwelling. Ravens nest on a ledge high above Long House and their droppings land on the site below.

And then of course there is the human animal. Although graffiti is not currently a big problem in Mesa Verde, it happens, so I had to learn techniques of infilling. Abrasion to erase graffiti is not acceptable because it creates a very noticeable fresh scar. More serious damage occurred while I was at Mesa Verde. Stones were broken and pushed over and a metate removed from the Mesa Top Loop sites. These problems have no easy solution. The metate was not replaced. The stones were glued back together and reset but the original fabric is now modified. A little bit of our past has been lost. One of the reasons the backcountry at Mesa Verde is not open to visitation is because of potential problems with vandalism and graffiti.

For those sites that are open to the public, a long-term problem is the oils on people's hands. Through the years, those features where hundreds and thousands of people place their hands – the doorway of the painted tower in Cliff Palace, many of the doorways in Balcony House – the stones and mortar have become noticeably darker and stained.

Safety is a major concern when the public is allowed to enter a site. It is important both that the public is safe when in a site, and also that the site is safe from the visitors. So the public never enters cliff dwellings without a park service employee, and obstacles and uneven surfaces are reduced as much as possible. The other big concern is hazardous rocks. The natural freeze-thaw cycle that created the alcoves is an ongoing process. Spruce Tree House has had special problems in this area but so have Long House and Step House. All the alcoves have had problems with spall rock over the years. Luckily, at least to my knowledge, no visitor or employee has been seriously hurt by falling rock, but it certainly could happen. In the 1970s a hazardous rock study was done in the park and just recently another one was done. In both cases nothing serious was noted.

THE TYPICAL SEASON

The field season for the stabilization crew typically started around the first of April with general housekeeping chores. Spruce Tree House is open all winter, so unless there was some other emergency situation, the first job was to do the housekeeping there. We swept the rooms and made any repairs that might be needed. Spruce Tree House is in a dry alcove so there are no weeds. In fact, dust in the covered kiva was the major chronic problem there.

Cliff Palace is the first cliff dwelling to open in the spring, so it was next on our list for housekeeping – sweep, weed, and do any repairs. Cliff Palace is in a wet alcove and some of the features are fairly exposed to rain, so weeding was as much a task as sweeping. The tunnel below the site was checked to make sure the water was flowing properly.

In a wet spring a lot of time might then be spent making sure drains around all sites were functioning. In a dry year we moved on to removing panels and raising curtains on the Mesa Top Road shelters and sweeping and weeding around those sites. We swept and weeded Fewkes Canyon sites (Oak Tree House, Fire Temple, New Fire House) that are visible from a distance. If major work was needed on a front-country site, an effort was made to tackle that before the June-September tourist season. During my tenure, there was some big project on the schedule almost every year.

Once the housekeeping, weeding and repairs were complete on Chapin Mesa, the crew then started the same process on Wetherill Mesa, which is open to the public from Memorial Day to Labor Day. We weeded and swept Long House and Step House, and Mug House if time allowed. Then we raised the curtains on the Badger House Community sites and swept and weeded around them.

As we weeded and swept, we always assessed the sites for damage that occurred over the winter. Once the housekeeping was done, then any needed repairs were addressed. Sometime in late May, window screening was put in place at Step House, over areas in Kiva A and elsewhere that bees were a problem.

By late spring weeds had started to grow around the open sites of the Far View area and Sun Temple so a lot of time was spent with hoe in hand. Once the weeds were under control, the crew addressed any major stabilization problems on the open sites on Chapin Mesa. There were always problems at these sites since they are exposed to the elements, so for a month or two in the summer Sun Temple, Far View House, Pipe Shrine House, and Coyote Village were repaired and re-pointed as needed.

The park had a program to re-point all the historic stone buildings. For a few years there was special funding for this program so a crew was hired just to work on historic buildings. But usually the main crew spent two weeks or more working on one of the 20-plus stone buildings in the park. By the time I left that was pretty much completed. It was considered easy duty. There were usually nice flat surfaces on which to erect scaffolding and all were an easy walk from a road so materials only had to be packed short distances. Two of the buildings had at one time been over-pointed with a portland cement mortar and work on those buildings was not such easy duty. The very hard mortar had to be carefully removed without damaging the stones. It was then replaced with a softer, more appropriate mortar.

With any luck there was time left to work in the backcountry on sites that needed some attention. I was frustrated by how hard it was to find time to assess the condition of backcountry sites, making it difficult to determine which were the most in need of repair. I spent time hiking to and assessing sites' conditions or a helicopter survey was made. Jack Smith, the chief park archaeologist for my first years, was quite familiar with the backcountry due to his earlier archaeological survey of the park, and he established areas to be targeted. For the most part I continued with his priorities once he retired. With recent increased special funding, there is now a program with staff to systematically assess and document backcountry cliff dwellings. It is a big project with well over 500 sites to photograph, map, and document with complete condition assessments.

During my years at Mesa Verde, we spent several weeks in September at Hovenweep National Monument as part of a multi-year program to stabilize the many structures there. Hovenweep is made up of five units, each containing towers, great houses, and room blocks, with many of the structures completely exposed to rain and wind. For most of the period that I was at Mesa Verde, Hovenweep was under the management of Mesa Verde, but it is now part of the southeast Utah cluster of parks and monuments and no longer part of the Mesa Verde stabilization program.

Once the work at Hovenweep was completed, it was time to pack up for projects outside the park. Through the years, the crew worked at Montezuma Castle, Chimney Rock, Glen Canyon, Kanab/Escalante-Grand Staircase, and Ute Mountain Tribal Park. These "outhouse" projects started in a year when there was not enough money to pay the crew for more than six months of work – the extent of the park service's obligation to permanent furlough staff – so I started looking around for outside projects. It added interest to the work, was great experience for everyone, and made a full eight-month season possible, April through November.

For our last month of fieldwork in November, it was back to Mesa Verde to roll down curtains and put on paneling at the mesa top shelters, check drainage around the sites for the last time, make sure Spruce Tree was still in good shape for winter visitors, and close down Cliff Palace. It was during my last check of Cliff Palace one season that I was horrified to find water flowing down a vertical crack in the back of the alcove.

End of season also entailed making sure all was well in Balcony House and the Fewkes Canyon sites and if it hadn't already been done, putting a fan and solar generator up on a Long House kiva. Also, Wetherill Mesa sites would be checked for the last time, making sure drains and shelters were fine.

The crew would then check out of their park housing and look forward to a winter with their families in Shiprock, New Mexico. They were typically on furlough for four months. During these winter months I wrote reports and cataloged hundreds of photographs. In a typical season the stabilization crew took about 50 rolls of 24-frame print film, and all 1,200

NATIONAL PARK SERVICE PROGRAMS

Like all government land-owning agencies, the National Park Service controls costs by squeezing individual parks' budgets. Maintenance declines until things get bad enough to draw the attention of visitors and members of Congress, and then a program is created to address some of the unmet needs. This cycle of alternating neglect and special programs extends throughout the National Park Service's 90-year history.

Several such programs have affected the preservation of resources in Mesa Verde National Park, including New Deal/Public Works Administration in the '30s, Mission 66 in the late '50s and early '60s, (special funding to revitalize deteriorating park facilities in anticipation of the park service's 50th anniversary), Project Rehabilitation in Parks (PRIP) in the '80s, and Vanishing Treasures and Save America's Treasures in the late '90s.

---

prints and negatives had to be entered into the park's photo catalog system. The task typically took me one month. I spent another two months writing reports on all the work done the past season. During the field season, I kept detailed daily notes on who worked, where we worked and who did what, the mortar mix and any other special materials involved as well as exactly what was done. If room size, condition, and features of the site had not previously been well documented, I did that. A designated person on the crew took "before," "during," and "after" photos of what each crew person was doing. Organized by site, the stabilization reports were a compilation of what we did, who did it, where it was done and why a particular action was taken. In the future these reports will make it possible to establish a stabilization history for every feature at every site, as well as track the history and success of a particular stabilization material in a particular environment.

I also worked on the following year's budget, considered new projects, and wrote grant proposals in the winter. It was rather easy to write a compelling grant proposal, given our great resources with high integrity, high visitation, much need, and status as a World Heritage Site. Once the excitement of receiving a grant was over, the obligations of budgets and report submittals took over. Special grants paid for tree ring research, the plaster preservation program, Balcony House report publication, my five-month stay in Rome studying preservation, and my research in the Nusbaum papers at the Smithsonian Institution in Washington, D.C.

NAVAJO, ANASAZI AND THE WHITE WOMAN

November 1998: Raymond recalls the day in Shiprock, in 1957, when his friend and fellow *Yeibichai* dancer Sam Yellowhorse asked him to dance at Coyote Canyon, New Mexico. Some of the dancers at Coyote Canyon were already working in maintenance or as trail crew at Mesa Verde. "Sam asked me if I was working somewhere. 'No,' I said. So he said, 'They need some crew at Mesa Verde and I want you to come work up there.' That's because I had done the *Yeibichai* with him. They had dances every night at the amphitheater in Mesa Verde, so he wanted a *Yeibichai* dancer. That's why he wanted me to work up there, so I told him, 'okay.' There wasn't work around here ... In the springtime ... Al Lancaster needed more men and asked Sam to get some ... We just went over there and Yellowhorse told Lancaster, 'This is the new crew.' Al Lancaster said, 'Okay, go to work'."

Nightly Navajo dancing at the park's campfire program stopped in the 1970s, over "some paperwork problem." The lead dancer didn't want to sign the paper.

Introduction

Slish, to, tse, the Navajo words flew through the air as a day of re-pointing passed – dirt, water, stone. These are the building blocks of the stabilization process through the vocabulary of the Navajo. Navajos dominated the stabilization crew during my stay in the park, but that is no longer the case. The last Navajo crew member retired in 2004. During my stay, my job was enriched by the constant contrasts between my cultural biases and those of the Navajo crew members. Navajo culture is much different from Pueblo, so although Native Americans were working on the cliff dwellings, these men did not consider themselves descendants of the cliff dwellers. They worked on the sites because they considered a job on the stabilization crew a good job, dependable, well-paid and relatively close to home. I liked them on the crew because they were good stonemasons, hard workers and returned year after year. They were also great people. The cultural difference between us was the frosting on the cake.

The Four Corners area of the American Southwest is, today, Navajo and Ute country. The Navajo Reservation dominates the region and tribal members dominate the population with more than 250,000 people on the tribal rolls. This wasn't always the case, at least if one relies on historic and archaeological data. Research places the *Diné*, the Navajo term for "the people," in the region at about the same time as the Spanish. At that time they were a small group of people who had acquired, or soon would, domesticated crops from the Pueblos. At about the same time they had their initial exposure to sheep and horses – two animals brought to the New World by the Spanish.

The *anasazi*, the Navajo term used to refer to the people who built the villages that dominate the landscape of Mesa Verde and much of the Navajo homeland, had moved away many years before the Navajo arrived.

DINÉ

The Navajo origin story places the *Diné* in the area between the four sacred mountains, Mt. Blanca to the east, Mt. Taylor to the south, the San Francisco Peaks to the west and Mt. Hesperus to the north, since the beginning of time.

The prevalence of Navajos in the early days of exploration for ruins in the Four Corners area led those explorers to adopt the Navajo term *anasazi* for the people who built the cliff dwellings and all the other ancient pueblos scattered over the landscape. Richard Wetherill is given credit for the adoption of the term, replacing the previous appellation of "Aztecs."

Fairly recently, some Pueblo groups – in particular the Hopi who are surrounded by the Navajo Reservation and are in conflict with the Navajo over land – have complained about the use of the term *anasazi*. They feel that the Navajo are stealing their history. But the Pueblo Indians speak many different languages, so there is not one term in use for their ancestors. Consequently, they suggest a combination of an English term and a Spanish term, Ancestral Pueblo, a rather unwieldy name. There are many people, who live away from the center of controversy in Hopi-Navajo country, who retain the use of the term *anasazi* for the people who built these early villages, pecked the petroglyphs, and built thousands of farming and water features across southern Utah and Colorado and northern Arizona and New Mexico.

Traditional Navajo Culture

At various times in the 17th and probably into the 18th century, pressures from the Spanish of the northern Rio Grande forced Pueblo Indians, then living along the Rio Grande and its tributaries, into contact with Navajos. Some Pueblos may have even lived with Navajo families for awhile. It was this contact that seems to have profoundly changed the Navajo economy from one based primarily on hunting and gathering to an economy based on farming and herding.

Some Navajo clans (a named kinship group based on descent through women) are from the Pueblo and suggest marriage between the two groups. But Navajo culture is not the same as Pueblo. Their language is different – related to the Apache languages, not to any of the Pueblo languages. The Navajo live spread out across the countryside, not in pueblos (the Spanish term for village). Their homes (hogans) are round and face east. Traditionally, Navajo practiced transhumance – moving seasonally between winter and summer pasturage. Pueblo farmers stay put and tend their fields year-round. Navajos take sweat baths, Pueblos do not. Navajos also practice a different religion – although it was greatly influenced by the Pueblos. Their religion emphasizes health while Pueblo religion is more concerned with the control of rain and fertility. Pueblos have an organized priesthood, religious societies, and an annual round of ceremonies. They focus on the common good, with the individual subordinate. Navajos have religious practitioners but no priesthood. Certain ceremonies take place at certain times of the year but there is not a fixed round of ceremonies. With the Navajo, an individual and his health problems are the reason for a ceremony. A sponsor and his kin group put on the ceremony.

The Navajo crew member from the most traditional community owns sheep that are kept in his mother's herd. He lives in Shiprock but his mother and several siblings live many miles to the east in the community where he was raised. He returns to his former home for ceremonies, and when he hosts a party in Shiprock, one of his sheep is brought to Shiprock and butchered. Navajos believe that every individual contains both good and evil and after death the evil component becomes a dangerous ghost. Also, certain natural phenomena can get out of harmony. Such things as snakes, coyotes, and lightning have a greater potential for evil than other things. The price one pays for an imbalance is illness, and the correct performance of a ritual is necessary to return to harmony. Most ceremonies are for curing disease, so religion and medicine are combined. Trained specialists, who have taken the time to learn one or more of the ceremonies, are hired to put on a ceremony. One finds a specialist informally by just "asking around." Most Navajos believe in witchcraft, defining a witch as someone who misuses ritual knowledge to do harm.

The clan is the basis of kinship for the Navajo, how they define themselves in relation to others. A Navajo is born into the clan of his or her mother, whether male or female. The father's clan is also important as the clan he or she is born for. Navajos consider themselves so closely related to people of their own clans that they would never marry within them, what anthropologists call clan exogamy. When one Navajo meets another, the first thing they establish is their kinship: What are your clans? This then defines how they will interact, for example as an aunt, brother, or potential mate. Clans are certainly not unique to the Navajo. In fact they are a very common, but not universal,

RESTORING HARMONY

On May 14, 1993, the southeast corner of the museum was struck by lightning at about 4:15 p.m. Chips of stone and mortar flew; stones were dislodged; the parapet and upper wall were damaged. Approximately 10 stones were shattered and several others dislodged. On Tuesday, May 18, after discussing the incident, one of the Navajo crew said to me, "Are you going to make us sick?" I didn't understand right away, but finally figured out he was concerned about working on a building that was struck by lightning. The park service sponsored a special Navajo ceremony June 3 to return harmony and allow the repairs to be made.

occurrence among American Indian groups and groups around the world.

The importance of clans varies among the Pueblo Indians, from very important to the Hopi to almost nonexistent in some Pueblo groups along the Rio Grande. The Navajo are expected to help their kin and residence group members. Interconnected relationships of descent and marriage carry certain responsibilities that are enforced by strong sanctions, and giving and receiving help is expected. Navajos respect individualism, but it is set in a communal environment of kinship and residence. They deplore coercion. Unanimity is the goal of decision-making within the residence group and at all higher levels.

The Navajo and Mesa Verde

The Navajo are associated with stabilization of Pueblo ruins because they are the group that now dominates the Anasazi homeland. At Mesa Verde this tradition started with the initial stabilization crew hired by Lancaster. But even earlier, Superintendent Nusbaum hired both *belagaanas* and Navajos to excavate ruins on his 1920s expeditions.

At Mesa Verde, the Navajos were, in fact, not only the closest source of laborers, but preferred over less reliable local workers by Nusbaum and later superintendents. There were no higher paying jobs back in Shiprock to lure them away. The Navajos became quite good friends with Nusbaum, but he took advantage of them in terms of salary, paying them less than *belagaanas*. The park did supply them with housing and wood for fuel. In their early years working in the park, the Navajo workers rode horseback or walked to the park and stayed for the season. Initially they lived in forked stick hogans located in what is now the picnic area on Chapin Mesa, and in the 1940s moved into stone hogans built by the park north of the picnic area.

A few Utes and many *belagaanas* have worked on the stabilization crew through the years but few have worked for more than a few years. It is the Navajo crew members that have returned year after year and made a career in stabilization. Al Lancaster is the only *belagaana* with a similar history. My 16 years don't even deserve a footnote. The crew chief during my stay worked there for 40 years. It is not surprising that Navajos have dominated the work force. They were, and maybe still are the largest group of unskilled laborers in the area and that is what the park was hiring – laborers. Navajos were hired to build roads, maintain ruins, and fight wildfires. They still work on park wildfire crews and maintenance crews. *Belagaanas* have always supervised the crew and functioned as the interface between the bureaucracy of the park service and the laborers who did the work. Even up to the end of the 20th century, the Navajos avoided paperwork as much as possible.

The Crew

Working with the Navajos on the stabilization crew was a wonderful experience for me. Not only were they great guys, but we all found our cultural differences fascinating. They were of course used to working around and for *belagaanas* but in no way were they assimilated into mainstream American culture.

I'm not sure when the tradition of a Navajo dance after the evening campfire program began. It was well established in the 1950s. One of the guys laughed that in the old days Navajos were hired not because they were good stonemasons but because they were good dancers. In the summer every evening after the campfire talk by a ranger, the Navajos would put on a small portion of a *Yeibichai* dance and then pass the hat. This all ended before my time in the park, when the superintendent apparently insisted that the head dancer sign some form and the group's organizer would not. Government demand met Navajo resistance over the issue of paperwork, and the dancing stopped.

In my time there was very little turnover of Navajos on the stabilization crew. Several who were seasonal workers when I started became permanent park service employees during my stay, and two younger Navajos were hired as seasonals. The core stabilization crew consisted typically of four permanent NPS employees and one seasonal. Of these, usually three or four were Navajos. The Navajos all lived in the Shiprock area – the Navajo town closest to Mesa Verde – and all were fairly traditional with the exception that wage labor had replaced sheep as the main source of income. Most had had very limited formal education. They could read and write but were not comfortable with understanding or filling out the endless forms that government employment required.

Several of the more recent Navajo employees found out about jobs from Navajos who were working on the crew. Another was working in maintenance and then moved over to stabilization. We always laughed about this because at the time this fellow was very thin and was supposedly hired because the crew needed someone to fit into vent shafts and other small spaces. Soon after being hired, he married and by the time he retired, he was lucky to fit through an *anasazi* doorway.

The crew members followed the standard Navajo patterns of etiquette. They would honk when they arrived at a person's home, and then wait for the person to come out. In greeting each other (and me) after an absence, they would shake hands with a very soft touch. To signal direction, they always used their lips. The Navajos were very concerned (one might say obsessed) with cleanliness and neatness. They cleaned their hands with dirt. Water was considered far too valuable to waste on hands when dirt would do. A *belagaana* on another park service stabilization crew who wore no socks, had long unkempt hair, and a pickup that looked like it had been in a war zone, was a sensation with the crew. The Navajos talked and laughed about him endlessly.

For the Navajo crew members, there were health problems that they went to physicians and hospitals to solve, and there were other problems that traditional medicine was better equipped to solve. *Belagaana* medicine was used

INTERVIEW WITH RAYMOND

November 1998

Kathy: "What was it like for you to work in a site where there were *anasazi* burials?"

Raymond: "If you do something ... step on, walk on, carry the bones, later it bothers you. The spirit. And then the medicine man will help you."

Kathy: "Did you feel that the bones would bother you?"

Raymond: "Well, maybe later. One Navajo on the crew, I know after he retired some years, he was getting sick so he had a ceremony. He was all right again, but he later died. I think it was [a] different [illness]."

for such problems as broken bones, cancer, or a heart attack. Medicine men were used for achy bones and general malaise. Their challenge seemed to be in figuring out which tradition best fit the problem. The Indian hospital in Shiprock is free to all Navajos, so a few of the crew used that first. Several of the Navajos did not like the hospital, so they paid to have the health insurance that is available to all permanent federal employees and consulted their own private doctor first. *Belagaana* medicine, public and private, was seen as less expensive than traditional, and so was often used first. When that didn't work, traditional medicine was used. But then certain things were seen as outside the interest and concern of *belagaana* doctors, including such things as sickness caused by lightning, snakes, or human bones.

The Navajos believed in ghosts (*chindi*) which, even of loved ones, are bad and can cause sickness. Human bones are related to ghosts, and so were carefully avoided. The Navajos never left their drinking water in a cliff dwelling overnight because a ghost might put something bad in it. The crew was also careful with their possessions because they could be used by an evil person to cast a spell on the owner. Skinwalkers are bad people. Once, when one crew member was drunk, he saw a skinwalker at night on his way home. It may be one reason he stopped drinking. Because of this concern for ghosts and skinwalkers, the Navajos did not like being out at night and thought I was crazy to walk my dog after dark.

On the other hand, the Navajos on the crew had no fear of heights (neither did the *belagaana* crew members). They had no problem with ladders, scaffolding, rappelling, or working near cliffs. Nor did they have a problem with motion sickness – in vehicles, helicopters, or boats.

Most of the Navajos on the crew had at one time in their lives had a problem with alcohol and all of the older members of the crew had type 2 diabetes, problems suffered by a very high percentage of all Native Americans. On the other hand, tobacco – a Native American narcotic – was not a problem for most. None of them smoked cigarettes, although one crew member did chew tobacco. Their diet was dominated by meat, including a lot of mutton and hamburger, beans, fried potatoes, bread and fry bread, diet sodas, apples and watermelon. At a celebration, a sheep or goat was butchered and everything was eaten – from blood (blood sausage) to brains to all the organs. They always took food to a ceremony, and for the host the idea was to have more food than could be eaten so everyone could take food home. This was a way to distribute food to a wide group of people but it made having a ceremony very expensive.

An interesting incident in the park emphasizes in a small way how cultures can be in conflict. An employee in the park decided to have a party for the stabilization crew among others. He bought steaks and was very put out when the Navajos left with the extra steaks he had purchased. In

---

IT WAS A GREAT PRIVILEGE FOR ME TO WORK WITH THESE MEN. THEY MIGHT HAVE PREFERRED A STRONGER, BIGGER PERSON, BUT I NEVER FELT DISCRIMINATED AGAINST BECAUSE I WAS A WOMAN.

---

another incident, I decided to invite the Navajo crew over to my campsite for dinner once when we were camping. I fixed steak and corn on the cob, but soon realized there was a problem. There was no bread, and for them a meal is not a meal without bread.

The men on the crew were very proud to be Navajo. They were also proud to be Americans and enjoyed such American pursuits as watching professional football and talking endlessly about their pickups. Only one was interested in acquiring ceremonial knowledge and then only after he retired. It was a great privilege for me to work with these men. They might have preferred a stronger, bigger person, but I never felt discriminated against because I was a woman. After all, the Navajo are a matrilineal society.

5

AN OBSESSION
WITH CLIFF DWELLINGS

Cliff Palace 2005.

esa Verde National Park is known for its cliff dwellings. These alcove villages were occupied for less than 100 years and make up only a small percentage of the archaeological sites found within the park. Yet they *are* the park to the average visitor. Of the approximately 600 cliff dwellings, only six will be discussed in depth here: the largest (Cliff Palace), the best preserved(Spruce Tree House), the two with the best documentation (Long House and Mug House), one with two visible periods of occupation (Step House), and one that is a challenge to enter (Balcony House). These sites have been excavated and stabilized and, with the exception of Mug House, are open to the public and the focus of the park's interpretive program. They were my obsession for 16 years.

D I R T ,   W A T E R ,   S T O N E   **69**

SPRUCE TREE HOUSE: THE "TYPE" SITE

May to October, evening: My dog barks at large blackbirds in flight or sitting in trees. She is trained well; she and I are a team. We look across Spruce Tree Canyon to see if there are any vultures roosting in the trees in front of the site. If there are, we bark, wave, and make noise to disrupt their repose and chase them down-canyon.

Introduction

Spruce Tree House is one of three cliff dwellings in Mesa Verde National Park with more than 100 rooms. Cliff Palace and Long House are the other two. Spruce Tree House has always been the centerpiece for the visitor experience. It is the only cliff dwelling open to the public year-round and the only one accessible to visitors in wheelchairs (although the trail does not meet the grade requirements for such designation). One of the great views in the park is from the porch of the ranger station, looking across Spruce Tree Canyon at this village. The Wetherill brothers named the village after trees growing in front, but in fact they are not spruce but Douglas fir. This was the first site in the park to be excavated and stabilized, in 1908 by Jesse Walter Fewkes. It was his "type" site, the one that would be used to interpret Pueblo architecture to the public.

History

Spruce Tree House was "discovered" by Richard Wetherill and Charlie Mason soon after Cliff Palace in 1888. Nordenskiöld was the first to

Spruce Tree House before stabilization. This photo was taken circa 1890s.

describe the site, in his classic work published in 1893. He took some great photographs and published the first plan map of the village.

Nordenskiöld really was a man before his time. When he was working in Spruce Tree House in 1891, he cut down a tree growing out of the wall of a kiva and counted the rings, thus establishing the latest possible date for use of the kiva. The tree's 167 rings meant that the kiva was at least that old, since it existed prior to the tree. It would be over 40 years before the development of tree ring dating established the actual date, the late 13th century.

Nordenskiöld examined some rooms in Spruce Tree House and removed a mat of plaited reeds and a small basket. He noted, as would others, the excellent state of preservation of the village. Like the other cliff dwellings he examined, he commented on the fact that there was no preplanned design. There was much evidence in wall abutments that the village was built and modified over time. The walkway that physically divides the village into two areas was obvious even without extensive excavation. He also could tell that several kivas were associated with each area. Turkey droppings in the back of the site suggested this was where they were kept. He described the rooms as small and rectangular and seldom over 7 to 10 feet. He noted that in some the walls were covered with soot; the walls in all kivas and some rooms were covered with a thin coat of plaster; and door-

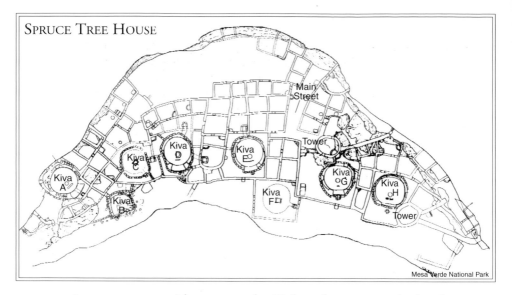

Kiva A

Kiva B

Kiva C

Kiva D

Main Street

Kiva E

Tower

Kiva F

Kiva G

Kiva H

Tower

Mesa Verde National Park

ways into rooms were either rectangular, T-shaped, or rectangular hatchways in the corner of room roofs. He speculated that the small rectangular doorways were for storerooms or other seldom entered rooms and the large T-shaped doorways were associated with rooms entered more often and so designed for easier use.

After Nordenskiöld it was another 17 years before the site was actually excavated and stabilized. Fewkes was brought from Washington, D.C., to tackle the first site excavation and stabilization two years after Mesa Verde became a national park in 1906. Legislation establishing the park specified that the area was to be preserved and interpreted and Fewkes very clearly set this as his goal. He chose Spruce Tree House as his first project because of the ready availability of water, with a very active spring in the head of the canyon, and because it was smaller and in better condition than Cliff Palace. At that time there were no roads into the park so personnel, tools, and non-local materials had to be brought in by horse to his camping area located above the site near where the present park museum and administration complex are situated. Fewkes' project took place in May and June with an appropriation of $2,000. His objective was the education of the public – to give them an idea of the features of a cliff dwelling by explaining "the meaning of the different parts, the construction and essential features of the rooms, their arrangement and special uses."

Fewkes identified 114 rooms in Spruce Tree House, of which eight were kivas. He numbered rooms and gave a letter designation to kivas, a tradition that has been maintained at Mesa Verde up to the present. He did not number upper-story rooms so only 72 numbered rooms appear on his published plan map. Kiva B, in front of the main portion of the site at the north end, was the only kiva Fewkes did not completely excavate. He noted that a "street" (labeled "main street" on his plan) divided the ruin in two and that the site was composed of several unit-type room clusters — the basic architectural unit of Pueblo society for hundreds of years over a huge geographic area. In 1903 and 1906 T.M. Prudden, a pathologist and southwestern archaeology enthusiast, published articles on his observation that small villages were scattered throughout the San Juan drainage, all of similar configuration with curved rows of rooms facing south or southeast, a kiva in front of the rooms, and a trash area in front of the kiva. He termed this a unit "pueblo." In Spruce Tree Fewkes observed that these units were arranged side by side with the addition of a wall connecting the row of rooms and encompassing the kiva. This wall formed one side of the enclosure and rooms formed the other three sides. He also noted that the shape of the units varied due to the shape of the alcove.

Tree ring dating and much more research has established that Prudden's unit pueblo is the early, basic unit of architecture for hundreds of years on the northern Colorado Plateau and surprisingly was lost once the Pueblo Indians left this area at the end of the 13th century.

Fewkes believed there were four units in Spruce Tree House, each associated with a row of rooms, kiva and courtyard. He believed the unit associated with Kiva A was the earliest and then three more units were added centering on Kivas C, E, and G. Then through time the units were enlarged with more rooms and a new kiva in each.

Fewkes was very concerned with interpreting the village to the public so he painted numbers on rooms and letters on kivas. He placed explanatory labels on features of Kiva G and labeled the three hand- and toe-hold trails near the site. He also rebuilt roofs over two kivas, C and F, using the roof design from two partially intact kiva roofs in Square Tower House. This gave the public an idea of the appearance of a courtyard and made it possible for the public to enter a kiva and see how it would have looked during occupation. A. Kidder (later a famous Southwest archaeologist) and Nusbaum, student workers with Hewett's Archaeological Institute of America in Santa Fe, were in the park the summer of 1908 and helped Fewkes. Nusbaum took many photographs of the site — before and after repairs — and Kidder helped with pottery analysis and the reconstruction of the kiva roofs. Fewkes believed reroofing the kivas was very important from an educational standpoint.

Fewkes believed the deflectors in kivas also functioned as altars and called the hole in the floor a sipapu, the Hopi term for the symbolic opening into the underworld found in their kivas. He had lived at Hopi prior to working at Mesa Verde, so it is not surprising that what he found at those pueblo villages in northern Arizona became the basis for interpreting what he found at Spruce Tree House. In Nordenskiöld's time the wall enclosing the site in the front was covered with fill. Fewkes excavated this area and stated that the wall was probably originally as high as a person's head. He did not rebuild it to that height undoubtedly so the public could actually see the village instead of just a high wall.

For some reason he did not mention that some of the kivas were connected to rooms by tunnels. He also didn't mention a second-story pillar which partially supports a third-story room, one of only two pillars in Mesa Verde cliff dwellings which support an upper-story room. (The other is in Spring House.) He also took no special note of the two towers in the south section of the site, one at either end of that cluster of rooms.

Nordenskiöld mentioned that there were no ladders in any of the cliff dwellings. Consequently there is no definite evidence that ladders were used to get to a site, from one section of a site to another, or from one story to the next. Fewkes brought up the problem of room entry where in some cases the doorways were so high that a ladder or notched log would be needed to reach them. But he also stated there was no evidence of either ladders or notched logs. He mentioned that some T-doorways had been modified with the lower portion filled, and that both T and rectangular doorways were sometimes completely filled. Doors were flat stones set in an adobe casing or held in place by a stick and door loops on the outside. One door was still in place when Fewkes worked at Spruce Tree House and remains there to this day.

Fewkes discussed the minor antiquities he found at the site. He believed it had been pretty thoroughly ransacked before he got there but considered the collection he made fairly representative. He sent the best and most easily portable of these objects to his institution, the National Museum. Based on the 18 whole or restorable vessels he recovered, he considered the occupants of Spruce Tree House expert potters. He didn't find any shell, turquoise or obsidian objects and concluded from this that trade was of little importance. He believed the isolation of the cliff dwellings, off the beaten trail of new ideas, resulted in conservatism in arts. Even at this early period he made a stab at using pottery designs for establishing culture areas, something 20th century archaeologists would spend hundreds of hours working to develop. Fewkes placed Mesa Verde in the San Juan area. Today his classification has been refined to separate the Northern San Juan or Mesa Verde area from the Chaco area, both subregions of the Anasazi. He found no evidence of the planting of cotton but lots of evidence for corn, beans and gourds. He speculated that pressure from outside tribes resulted in the location of villages in alcoves.

Stabilization

Fewkes' project included not only excavation but also stabilization of Spruce Tree House. His work here and earlier at Casa Grande in Arizona was some of the earliest stabilization in the Southwest. Unfortunately, his lack of documentation has made later preservation of Spruce Tree House difficult. Fewkes used the same materials in his repairs (resetting original stones in a reconstituted mud mortar) as were used by the original builders. For this reason it is not always clear what is his work and what is truly original. He identified water cascading over the alcove onto walls in the village as the most destructive force affecting the village. He dealt with this by "blasting" a trench into the slick rock above the site, 254 feet long, two feet deep, and three feet wide, diverting water to either end of the alcove. Fewkes also improved the trail to the site and built a trail through it.

In the 1920s falling rock destroyed the roof of a restored kiva (probably Kiva F); presumably this damage was repaired. In 1934 this roof was rebuilt at the same time some major stabilization was done in the north and central portions of the site with funds from the Public Works Administration.

In my years at Mesa Verde, Spruce Tree House was, fortunately, one of the few sites that required very little attention. Fewkes rebuilt the roofs over two kivas and in 1932 Superintendent Finnan roofed another kiva. Because Spruce Tree is located in a dry alcove (lacking a spring and therefore spared the constant water issues of wet alcoves), these kivas have been remarkably stable. Dust is the biggest problem, predominantly in the only kiva entered by visitors, because it is enclosed and has high visitation. The stability of the three roofed kivas in Spruce Tree House is in stark contrast to what has happened to a roofed kiva in Long House, a wet alcove. Moisture trapped in the enclosed Long House kiva has turned many of the original wall facing stones to sand.

The instability of the alcove has been the major preservation problem at Spruce Tree House since it was first noted by Al Lancaster in 1940. Lancaster spotted two cracks in the sandstone above the site creating a nearly detached arch. Geologists and engineers were called in from the regional office and installed gauges to monitor the cracks. They recommended removing rocks and vegetation on the mesa top above Spruce Tree and covering the area to keep out snow. The crack was cleaned and filled with emulsified asphalt where it was narrow at its ends and roofed over and waterproofed in the wider sections; a framework of steel rods bridged the crack every 12 inches. Then metal lath was placed over the rods and covered with tar paper. The tar paper was tucked into a 3-inch-wide groove cut along the upper edge of the crack, secured with metal lath and painted with asphalt sprinkled with gravel. Then six times through the 1940s, again in 1952 and 1960, the crack was resealed.

By 1955 the kiva in front of the north end of the site, Kiva B, which had only been partially excavated by Fewkes, was a weed-filled hole, so it was excavated. Because the kiva was in poor condition, not well protected by the alcove and in the way of visitor traffic, it was backfilled after the excavation. That same year the trail in front of the north end of the village was raised two feet so it would be easier for the public to see over the retaining wall into Courtyard C-D.

In March 1960 a major rockfall destroyed a portion of the retaining wall enclosing Kiva H, 60 feet of visitor trail and portions of the front retaining wall. There was also some damage to Kiva F. Several of the boulders from this fall were so solidly embedded that they were left in place. One example

Pinning cliff above Spruce Tree House in 1962.

is the large boulder just south of Kiva F near the park service bench. Luckily this incident occurred at night so no one was hurt. The park service repaired the retaining wall around Kiva H and the trail. Long poles were used to remove loose spalls and sandstone flakes from the ledges and alcove roof above the site and a 5-ton slab was winched off. Later in the same year the lip of the alcove over the site fractured and partially detached a slab of rock, creating an arch over the site. In 1961-62 an Ohio company was hired to anchor the loose slab with bolts and grout. They also anchored a second detached arch and removed two large sections of cliff face that were loose.

A copper lip was installed in 1961 to divert water away from the area of the alcove roof where rock had dislodged. Drainage channels were chiseled into the bedrock above the site to divert water away from the sealed crack and over to the area with the copper lip. After studying the arch in 1964-65, the U.S. Geological Survey recommended that loose slabs and blocks of rocks be removed, that additional bolts be added, that runoff water be better controlled, and that the area be regularly monitored. In 1964 another sandstone slab fell from the roof of the alcove at the north end of the site, but did not cause any damage. In that year the stabilization crew completely cleared the mesa top above the site, cleared drainage ditches of debris, enlarged one ditch, sprayed the mesa top with a waterproofing chemical, and treated the drainage ditch with an epoxy grout. Since the 1960s the Spruce Tree House alcove has been stable, thankfully. A hazardous rock study in 1978 revealed no serious rock hazards and more recent monitoring has also suggested that the alcove is stable.

When I began work on the stabilization crew, the alcove had been stable for well over 15 years. There was sketchy documentation and almost no institutional memory of all that had been done to stabilize it. I was told in general of the problem or at least heard my supervisor discussing it with others. A history of stabilization of Cliff Palace and Spruce Tree House was written by a park contractor in 1988. For the first time, park records were organized and their report documented the problems with the alcove over Spruce Tree House. Sadly, information on the exact application techniques and the recommended maintenance and reapplication cycles was never found. So for the most part, during my tenure we cleaned the ditches above the site very faithfully but did not apply any chemicals, re-grout, or re-tar. It may have been just luck, but during my tenure the alcove remained stable.

Because of the drainage ditches, the water patterns around the site have changed dramatically in the last 100 years. Much of this water now falls in front of the site at both the north and south ends of the alcove, where it has caused erosion of the midden and retaining walls. A section of the retaining wall at the north end of the site was repaired in 1985 and again in the '90s when I was in charge of the project.

To prevent further collapse, I decided to place a scupper at the end of the drainage ditch above the site, which would force the water to fall in front of the retaining wall. It seemed like a win-win situation since the modification would have no direct impact on the site and would get the water away from the wall supporting the visitor trail and site midden. It was fairly easy to build and put in place. Unfortunately I had not thought through the impact this approach would have on the landscape. With the bedrock above the site so devoid of vegetation, the scupper is very visible. No one has ever said anything to me about the impact on the landscape but at least to me there definitely was a negative effect. I can always tell if a photograph of Spruce Tree alcove was taken before or after the scupper was installed in 1997. Another scupper, at the south end of the site and in place before my time, is not nearly as noticeable because it is not right over the site and is partially screened by vegetation.

Over the years the dusty trail in front of the site has been a concern. Park officials decided against using asphalt right in front of the cliff dwelling, but here as elsewhere portland cement mixed with dirt (called a soil cement) has been used to reduce dust and the rate of erosion of the visitor trail. Enough dirt is used in the mix that the resulting surface is the color of the non-amended dirt in the alcove. But even these hardened surfaces eventually wear unevenly and have to be replaced. One joy of working in Spruce Tree House is that a small garden tractor can be used on the trail to get materials into and out of the site. During my tenure, several projects to repair worn areas of the trail took place in the village.

Recent Research

In the years after Fewkes, the National Park Service seemed to agree with him that there was little to learn from such a looted site. But that was definitely wrong, and in the last 10 years or so some very interesting research has been done in the village. Rock art and early inscriptions have been inventoried. The earthen plaster which is on so many of the walls has recently been documented and its condition assessed.

Another important addition to our knowledge of the site was the recent comprehensive sampling of wood for tree ring dating. Working before the development of tree ring dating, Fewkes had no idea when the site was built and occupied, no room construction dates, no way to compare construction of the various areas of the site except by a close examination of the bonding and abutment of walls. Even that was unreliable, since abutting walls could have been built hours apart or generations apart. The first tree ring samples were removed from the site in 1923. More were taken in 1932 and 1941, for a total of 36 samples, but for a site with hundreds of in situ roof beams this was a shockingly small sample of the datable wood. Only in the past 12 years has the wood in the site been completely sampled. Now there are a total of 262 dated samples from Spruce Tree House.

We now know that the site was built between 1210 and the 1270s. The current head of the stabilization program at Mesa Verde has been documenting Spruce Tree House for several years and concludes that the village

Vultures on cliff above Spruce Tree House.

Mesa Verde National Park

was built primarily between the 1230s and 1270s with the earliest structure still intact built in 1210. This room was then abandoned and finally repaired or remodeled in 1271. For the site as a whole, eight rooms were built in the 1230s, 11 rooms and two kivas in the 1240s, 14 rooms and one kiva were added in the 1250s, and seven rooms were built in the 1260s. There was a building boom in the 1270s, with 12 rooms constructed just before final abandonment around 1280. The south end of the site has yet to be incorporated into this study.

The Vulture Problem

Vulture: *a big black bird with a red featherless head.*

They are a common bird over the park in the summer. In the morning they can be seen, with their wings spread, basking in the sun on the slickrock above Spruce Tree House. In the late afternoon they are languidly flying in that same area, getting ready to alight for the evening on a fir tree branch. Once in the trees they bounce around a bit, settling in for the night. This is their roost. During the day they disperse, flying high over the park.

Often visitors think these high flying big birds are eagles, only to be uniformly disappointed when their true identity is revealed. They shouldn't be. These are great birds. I watched them every season for just under 20 years – on early morning and early evening walks with my dog or anyone else that would go along. These fair-weather visitors arrive in the park in late March and leave in October. They eat carrion but I never saw one hovering around road kill as I have in California; I don't know why.

During the day they seem to stay away from the heavily visited areas of the park but in the evening they return to their roost near Spruce Tree House.

My interest in vultures became much more complex in 1992 and lasted until I left the park in 2002. In 1992 the vultures that had been roosting either down-canyon from Spruce Tree House or in some cases in the trees in front of the site started roosting on the walls of the village. The birds sit for awhile in one place and then bounce to another until they finally settle in for the night. The birds were doing their final bounce onto the walls well after my evening walk. Interpretive rangers that work in the site during the day reported the problem. The smell of the fresh excrement on the walls of the site was quite noticeable in the heat of the afternoon.

Thus began an effort to convince these birds to roost down-canyon from Spruce Tree House. Park naturalist, interpretive rangers, and stabilization crew – we all got involved. And despite our efforts, I think the birds still won. We tried helium balloons, fake owls, and noise. And although all of this worked in the short term, we did not find a long-term solution. In Cliff Palace I placed Slinkies on walls to discourage birds (in this case not vultures) but in Spruce Tree I decided the spring-like toys would be too visible. Balloons and owls worked fine except they had to be put in place every night and removed before the site was open to visitors every morning. Any slacking off and the birds would return. Noise was easier than – and just as good as – balloons and owls, but again we had to be persistent.

Every evening my dog and I would stand on the slickrock across from Spruce Tree House and make noise to frighten the birds coming in to roost, trying to convince them to move down-canyon. Then in the early morning we would check again to see if any had returned after our noise-making the night before. If they had, we would wake these birds up with our displeasure. Our efforts would go on all summer until the birds left the park in October. But of course on days when I was out of the park... Persistence pays. As far as I know, no one is even checking on the vultures late in the evening now. My replacement on the stabilization crew does not live in the park, and I don't know if the interpretive rangers have started complaining again.

There is a second problem with the vultures as well, one that I really made no effort to address even though it did have an effect on me and our program. They often lay their eggs in cliff dwellings – none that are open to the public but in some of the cliff dwellings in the back country. Vultures do not build a nest. They lay their eggs amidst the rubble on the floors of rooms. Their white excrement accumulates in these "nesting" areas over the years, not only disfiguring the walls and displacing stones, but also causing a smell after years of accumulation that is almost overwhelming and makes working in these areas very unpleasant. Also the eggs and chicks can be found in these rooms during the height of the backcountry stabilization season.

This happened on Moccasin Mesa. We were working on several small sites in the area and when we came to the last one, there was a chick in a room next to the one on which we needed to make repairs. We did not enter the room with the chick, since no work was needed there. But we did work on the room next door. I returned weeks later to document the chick's room and found it dead. I was upset that our activities might have resulted in the mother abandoning her chick. So later that season when I noted chicks in another cliff dwelling, I decided not to work in the site, but rather to wait and do the repairs early the next season before nesting. Unfortunately by then one of the walls in the site had collapsed. Nothing good came of my association with nesting vultures.

Conclusion

Spruce Tree House is the perfect cliff dwelling. It is in a dry alcove and so it is the best preserved of all the major cliff dwellings. Even vultures seem to admire the original high walls. Fewkes' type site is the place to view rows of intact doorways, plastered walls extending up three stories, roofed kivas set in their courtyard, a second-story pillar holding up an upper room, and plastered walls graced with dots and triangles and a rectangular design. The walk to the site takes visitors under a beautiful stand of fir trees and past a very reliable spring. It is easy to envision living in Spruce Tree village and to make this even easier, a diorama in the museum shows Spruce Tree village as it would have looked as a functioning village with kids and turkeys and dogs and pots.

Don Ross

Spruce Tree House diorama.

CLIFF PALACE: THE ICON

November 1995: My worst nightmare. I'm in Cliff Palace spreading mothballs to discourage rodents. The field season is over and the last activities are
taking place to close the sites for winter. Then I hear: drip, drip, drip. Water
is dripping onto room walls from a crack in the roof of the alcove.

Introduction

Every visitor to Mesa Verde National Park has either seen pictures of this
village or heard about it. It is the cliff dwelling everyone wants to visit,
with its amazing size and spectacular setting. Cliff Palace contains the
greatest number of rooms (rooms, kivas and open areas) of any cliff
dwelling. It is this dense clustering of rooms within a large 80-foot by 20-
foot alcove, at various levels on the sloping floor, which appeals to all –
undoubtedly to the original builders as much as to modern visitors.

Like all Mesa Verde cliff dwellings, this is not a preplanned village.
Rooms were added, abandoned, and modified throughout its occupation.
The village as it appears today dates to the late 13th century. There are
depressingly few tree ring dates, considering the size of the site, but the
cutting dates from the wood that does exist are in the 1260s and 1270s.
The main portion of the site is on the sloping floor of the alcove. There are
also 10 rooms on a natural ledge above the very back portion of the main
village and a kiva within a tower outside the alcove to the west.

Cliff Palace is the largest village in a cluster of cliff dwelling villages.
Sunset House and Swallows' Nest are down-canyon. Balcony House is
across the mesa to the east, and Oak Tree House, New Fire House and Fire
Temple are across the canyon to the west. Besides these sites, there are

82 AN OBSESSION WITH CLIFF DWELLINGS

numerous smaller cliff dwellings in the area. Also right across Cliff Canyon, on the mesa top, is Sun Temple, a late 13th century ceremonial site.

The question of whether there was enough water for all of the people who lived in the area is an important one. The occupants of Cliff Palace needed water for daily consumption, and for their periodic construction. In 1911, Jesse Fewkes found the alcove dry. He "developed a good supply [of water] in the canyon below the ruin" but exactly where that would have been and what he meant by "developed" is not known. There is a very dependable spring across Cliff Canyon from Cliff Palace, at the mouth of Fewkes Canyon, and seeps at the top of the talus at the contact of sandstone-shale lenses both north and south of Cliff Palace.

History of an Icon

Gustaf Nordenskiöld visited Cliff Palace in 1891. He created a plan of the unexcavated site identifying over a hundred rooms including 17 kivas. He took numerous photographs of the site and noted two kivas that differed in construction from the typical form, being square with rounded corners. Although not mentioned by Nordenskiöld, they also do not have pilasters and in fact there is no evidence that they were ever roofed. None of the artifacts illustrated in Nordenskiöld's publication on the cliff dwellings is from Cliff Palace, so quite possibly all the museum-quality objects had been removed before his visit. The absence of structural wood throughout this site was so dramatic that it was noted by Nordenskiöld.

Cliff Palace was the second cliff dwelling excavated and stabilized after the creation of the park. Fewkes returned to the park in 1909 to excavate and repair Cliff Palace with an appropriation of $4,360. The project took from May through August. His report on this work is brief and primarily descriptive. He felt there was no way to reconstruct the life of the people who had lived in the village, blaming the lack of undisturbed deposits and the site's poor state of preservation, with no wood remaining and many walls broken down. Fewkes felt that no cliff dwelling in the Southwest had been more thoroughly dug over in search of pottery and other objects

TECHNOLOGICAL KNOWLEDGE

Recent research by conservators found evidence of powder used in explosives on Cliff Palace plaster. Such modern equipment as electron microscopes, digital cameras, laser technology, and sophisticated computer programs have made it possible to look more closely at plasters, mortars, and construction technology. We now know the mineral composition of plasters and mortars, layer thickness and texture. The field is changing rapidly and although I don't believe it is yet possible to localize the work of individual masons, that time may come.

CEMENTING CLIFF PALACE

There is no remaining evidence of Fewkes' cement in Cliff Palace. It apparently was only used to cap walls, and now in those exposed areas where capping is needed (such as Kivas A and B) stone is used. Most of these stones are set in a concrete mortar but this work is all of more recent date. Fewkes left the trail into and out of the alcove much the same as the one used by the early explorers, but did create a trail through the site for the use of visitors. The wall dividing Cliff Palace into two parts was modified to enable visitors to cross from one part to the other.

for commercial purposes. Walls had been broken down with explosives, often simply to let light into the darker rooms; floors were damaged and buried kivas mutilated. Openings had been blasted into the walls which form the front of the ruins just to get rid of debris. Beams were used for firewood to so great an extent that not a single roof remained. This destruction, plus erosion due to torrents of rain, left Cliff Palace in a sad condition, according to Fewkes.

During Fewkes' excavation and stabilization, the site was mapped with rooms numbered and kivas identified by letter. He concentrated on repairing wall foundations and the damage done to walls by early uncontrolled digging. He reconstructed the corner of the four-story painted "tower" (with the third-story room plastered and decorated) at the south end of the site. A volunteer assistant, R.G. Fuller, photographed and surveyed the site during this project. In Fuller's account of the work, he commented on the use of portland cement, the first use of this material in a cliff dwelling and possibly the first use in ruins stabilization in the Southwest.

> There was one good feature in the rains, for they showed us where the drip came on the ruins and enabled us to lay Portland [*sic*] cement where it would be most effective. It was the only possible way of saving the walls in many places, and while it was not in keeping, it was decidedly better than allowing things to fall to pieces.

So portland cement was used but not indiscriminately. It was used where an earthen mortar would be ineffective and there was an obvious concern that the finished product was not "in keeping" with the original workmanship. It is curious that there was no attempt to direct water from the masonry walls by construction of drainage channels above the ruins, as Fewkes had done at Spruce Tree House.

Fewkes identified two main types of rooms, ceremonial and secular, with two subtypes of ceremonial rooms and six subtypes of secular rooms. Of the ceremonial rooms, the presence or absence of a roof was used to

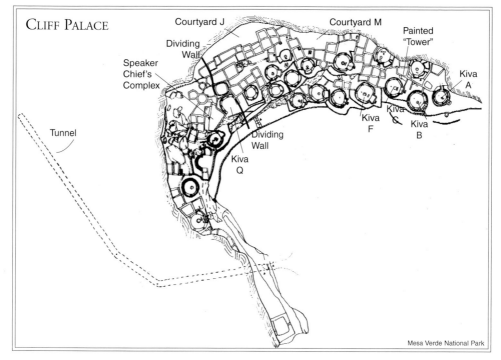

CLIFF PALACE

Courtyard J

Dividing Wall

Speaker Chief's Complex

Courtyard M

Painted "Tower"

Kiva A

Tunnel

Dividing Wall

Kiva Q

Kiva C

Kiva F

Kiva B

Mesa Verde National Park

make a distinction between types. Most of the kivas (19) had pilasters which supported the roof. One kiva was an exception but since it was roofed (the upper walls undoubtedly supported the roof), it was placed in this category for a total of 20 kivas with roofs. Three circular, subterranean rooms did not have pilasters and there was no evidence they were ever roofed and so these were placed in his second subtype.

In the text of his report Fewkes mentioned finding a great deal of broken pottery which he classified as coiled and indented, or smooth polished. The illustrated objects from his excavation include black on white bowls, two black-on-white kiva jars, a corrugated jar, two mugs, a dipper, stone ax with handle, six ax heads, three pot rests, a basket, numerous sandals, numerous bone awls, planting sticks, and a woven tumpline. He found two pieces of turquoise, a fragment of a *tchamahia* which in a footnote he stated was used on an altar at the Hopi village of Walpi. He stated that the objects uncovered at Cliff Palace were similar to those found at Spruce Tree House. Some or all of these objects were sent to the National Museum.

As with Nordenskiöld, Fewkes was convinced the cliff dwellers were related to the Pueblo Indians and throughout the publication compared what he found at Cliff Palace with the situation in the Hopi villages. Although interested in the placement of Cliff Palace in time, he could only speculate on the temporal relationship of Cliff Palace to that of neighboring villages, such as Spruce Tree House, and the ruin across the canyon on the mesa top (Sun Temple). He wondered whether the kiva-room ratio differed through time. At

Cliff Palace there were seven secular rooms to every kiva while at Spruce Tree House there were 15 to every kiva. Comparing this to modern Pueblos where there are many more secular rooms than kivas, he concluded that Cliff Palace was older than Spruce Tree House. We now know because of tree ring dates that Cliff Palace and Spruce Tree House as well as all the other cliff dwellings are basically of the same age.

Fewkes found no evidence of a cataclysm at the end of the occupation, and so believed that the final abandonment of the Mesa Verde was the result of an unfavorable environment. The argument is still being used to explain the movement of people out of the San Juan River drainage. It is now known that there was a drought in the late 13th century.

Research and Stabilization after Fewkes

Cliff Palace was sampled for tree ring material by the First Beam Expedition in 1923 and by the University of Arizona's Laboratory of Tree-Ring Research in 1931-32. The dates were first published in 1935. Even with the limited number of dated samples, it was clear that the site was 13th century.

From 1909 to 1934 there is no record of any other research or repairs to the features of Cliff Palace. A drainage trench was excavated into the rimrock above the site in 1932. Then in 1933 Public Works Administration (PWA) funds were allocated for the mapping, documentation and repair of Cliff Palace and other cliff dwellings. Earl Morris was in charge of the project but it was Al Lancaster who did the on-site supervision. During this project, which started in 1934, the north end of the site was photo-documented and mapped in detail, the boulder upon which the Speaker Chief's complex was built was stabilized with a steel I-beam and concrete, the repairs then covered with a veneer of stone. Wooden roof beams from Balcony House across the mesa and Aztec Ruins in New Mexico were added to the rooms making up the Speaker Chief's complex to stabilize walls. Also the corner of the four-story painted "tower" was rebuilt due to the poor quality of Fewkes' reconstruction.

Trails

Cliff Palace has been the "crown jewel" of park interpretation since the park's founding. Hundreds and now thousands of visitors enter the site annually. Initially visitors walked through the site and staff spent a lot of time controlling dust. In 1939 the visitor trail was moved to the front of the site and after World War II visitors were restricted to this trail. This reduced visitors' physical contact with the structure and led to better preservation of plaster and wall mortar.

Through the years the dirt trails in the site were surfaced with concrete, both the trail in front of the site and the trail as it circles Kivas A, B, C and F at the south end of the site. Huge cracks in the surface of the concrete trail in front of the site prompted its replacement in the early '90s. The trail was slipping down-canyon and the resultant cracks were a hazard to those walking on it. In some areas this pad was replaced with stones (areas where the surface was being hit by runoff) and in others a packed clay/silt/sand mixture was used with a color that blended in with the color of the site's sandstone walls.

The concrete pad around the kivas was fairly stable so I didn't think much about it until a fabric conservator pointed out the moisture and deterioration occurring in the stones, mortar and bedrock around it. Once it was pointed out, it was obvious. The impermeable concrete trail had to be removed because it was forcing all moisture through wall stone or bedrock boulders, accelerating deterioration of original materials. In the last few years before I left, the crew replaced all of this concrete with a surface that can let moisture evaporate naturally – again a compacted soil path. I never did figure out exactly when the concrete had been laid. It was undoubtedly done to reduce

---

OVER THE YEARS THE OILS FROM PEOPLE'S HANDS HAD DISCOLORED THE STONES AND MORTAR TO A VERY DARK BROWN.

---

the amount of mud on the tourist path, seal surfaces to rain, and control dust.

For the crew this concrete replacement project was a nightmare. All the concrete had to be carefully broken up and pulled by rope and pulley out of the site. Then new soil had to be lowered into the site. Cliff Palace is open through almost the whole stabilization season, so there was really no time to get into the site when it was closed to the public. Our window of opportunity was early in the morning and what wasn't finished then was done between tour groups. In 2004 when I entered Cliff Palace for the first time in several years I was very excited to see that the dampness that once could be seen in the walls at the south end of the site was now a thing of the past. There was no question, though, that now with a compacted soil trail, more time would be needed each year to repack eroded areas. But never again would concrete chunks have to be removed from the site. The eroded soil can be just swept over the edge of the alcove.

Another project was the removal of staining from stones and mortar along the public trail by the painted "tower." Over the years the oils from people's hands had discolored the stones and mortar to a very dark brown. To someone who visits the sites regularly and is familiar with old photographs, this problem was obviously getting worse with increased visitation after World War II. The same problem existed in Balcony House and Spruce Tree House, wherever there were lots of hands and readily available stones and mortar to touch. Again an architectural fabric conservator recommended ammonium chloride (sold as Fantastic, a household cleaner). He suggested wetting the area, spraying on the chemical, and then using a wet, absorbent paper to wick out the oils. This didn't work very well but a gentle scrub of the sandstone and mortar and then a damp cleaning was effective. The staining didn't go away but color of the area did lighten and blend in better with the surrounding unstained areas.

The real answer to this problem is to have all visitors wear gloves when they are in the cliff dwellings, similar to wearing cotton booties in historic houses. People would get their own pair when buying tickets. They could even have a Mesa Verde pottery design on them, a souvenir of their visit. This will come some day although I must admit that no one took my idea very seriously when I suggested it.

Water

All through the 90-year history of preservation of Cliff Palace, it is important to remember that dry areas of the site have needed very little attention. Those areas that are not protected by the alcove have needed lots of stabilization and that is where cement mortars have been used to retain the form of the walls. In these exposed areas few original floor features remain and most of the stones have been reset in a portland cement mortar.

Although Fewkes specifically mentioned that he did not find water in Cliff Palace, it is problems brought on by water *in* the alcove that have dominated the preservation history of this site. Water entering through seeps and cracks prompted excavation for placement of drain pipes in 1948, construction of a tunnel in 1961, and abandonment of flush toilets and water fountains in the visitor parking lot in the 1990s.

By the 1940s, moisture was mentioned as a serious problem in Cliff Palace. It is not clear when the problem started or where it occurred within the site. In 1943 water was blamed for the collapse of a kiva wall and in 1946 there was mention of a water problem in the painted "tower" section of the site. The collapse and settling of the front retaining and terrace walls below Speaker Chief's complex in 1948 resulted in the placement of 35 feet of drainpipe below grade behind the base of the wall. Then in 1949 water-saturated sand and stones were removed from the small ledge above the central portion of the site. With all of these moisture problems and after much debate and input from outside experts, the decision was made to excavate a tunnel "under" the site to intercept the water at the shale/sandstone contact. To intercept the ground water before it entered the site, a consulting geologist recommended a 300-foot tunnel be excavated at the contact of sandstone and shale where ground water flowed. This was done from June through August 1961 with Mission 66 funds.

The drainage construction was so successful that the north end of the

Cliff Palace, January 1996.
Note the buckets and hoses that are catching water and moving it to the front of the alcove.

site is now relatively dry. A steady stream of water goes through the tunnel, which is actually north of the alcove village, with its mouth below the site. (See plan of site.)

At the same time this seep water was being diverted and the north end of the site was drying out, another moisture problem was in the making. Water for flush toilets and a drinking fountain was brought to the visitor parking area above Cliff Palace with other Mission 66 funds. Almost as soon as the restrooms were opened, park staff noted that while the tunnel was successful in drying up the north end of the site, effluent was saturating the south and central portions of the site. Initially the wastewater, septic tank, and leach field were the problem, as the treatment area wasn't designed to deal with the amount of flow. The system to deal with the effluent was redesigned and rebuilt in 1960 and again in the 1980s.

Then in the fall and winter of 1995-96, hundreds of gallons of water flowed down a crack (which follows a fault) onto walls and floors in the back of the Cliff Palace alcove. I was down in the site spreading mothballs to discourage rodents before the Thanksgiving holiday, right after the crew had left for the season, when I heard water dripping. It was obviously an unusual amount of water and it only got worse through the winter. Water saturated sandstone, mortar, plaster and fill. Plaster washed off walls; mortar became saturated and lost its ability to bond; and sandstone turned soft. Water means loss and lots of water means lots of loss. My call for help very quickly brought many hands and heads to solve the immediate problem. A complex of buckets, pipes, and sheet plastic was used to capture at least most of the water and get it to the front of the site where it was released into Cliff Canyon.

It was also important to figure out why this was happening. In fact we discovered that a leaky pipe underneath the parking lot above the site had broken and was not repaired. This had been going on all summer. By November the area was so saturated that water was standing in puddles in the parking lot. Also, an overflow valve had been left on to maintain the proper chlorine level for drinking water. Apparently since Cliff Palace was at the end of the waterline there was a problem with water quality. The water line was turned off and the restrooms closed. This was always done in the winter anyway, but now it was permanent. Flush toilets have been replaced by pit toilets.

This water problem has led to the most recent research at Cliff Palace. Water-damaged sections of the site, Courtyards J and M, were the most intensively studied. A basic construction sequence for the entire site also was developed and all wood in the structure was documented and sampled if of appropriate size for dating. I decided that no stabilization was necessary in this area damaged by water. It is not visible to the public, and despite the loss of plaster and much mortar, the walls are still supporting their own weight.

A final water problem still lurks over Cliff Palace. Mission 66 funds were used to enlarge the parking lot above Cliff Palace in the 1960s. This huge, paved area was then sloped to drain into the ditch right above the site. This ditch follows a crack in the bedrock, a crack that extends all the way down into the alcove. And it is here where water was dripping on that nightmarish day in November 1995. Much of that water in 1995 was due to the broken waterline and the open water valve, but much of the residual moisture along the crack is undoubtedly due to the parking lot design.

It is interesting that before the big water problem in November 1995, I knew there was moisture in the back part of the site near the center of the complex but I just accepted it as background noise, something that just *was*. Once the dripping started and research into the history of water problems in Cliff Palace was initiated, it became clear that the damp area which I had come to accept had at one time been dry. That is when the waterline and parking lot design took on new interest, and the relationship was identified between the ditch/fault above the site and the crack in the alcove – they are one and the same.

Two points became obvious after this crisis. First, it is critical to know the history of a site to be able to spot new problems. Second, it is critical to be careful when any change is made to a fragile environment – whether it is drinking water, toilets and a paved parking area or the introduction of concrete trails for visitors. Without thinking through the implications, damage might very well occur to the site. Once that damage is done, it cannot be undone. Stones and mortar can be replaced but it will never be original again. The integrity of the site has been reduced. Interestingly, this really matters to people. One of the most common questions visitors ask is how much of the site is real, how much dates back to the time of the original builders. Luckily in both Spruce Tree and Cliff Palace much of the fabric is original. Spruce Tree House has more original fabric than Cliff Palace and one reason is that Cliff Palace has endured so many water problems over the years.

Recent Research

After the 1930s, almost no research was done on Cliff Palace. Fewkes' report was short and descriptive but there seems to have

NEVADA BARR AND CLIFF PALACE

Maybe everyone that lives long enough finds among their acquaintances a person who has become famous. For those of us who lived at Mesa Verde in the early 1990s that person is Nevada. She was one of several seasonal rangers, the cops of the park. She was friendly and compassionate, didn't give the other staff lots of speeding tickets and such. She certainly liked animals and several times brought back my walk-about dog after one of her break-outs. At that time I had no idea Nevada was an aspiring mystery writer. I wish I had. After reading *Ill Wind*, which in fact is very good, I wished I had talked to her about the tunnel under Cliff Palace. That would have added to her story line and, of course, the tunnel is true.

been the feeling in the park service that there was nothing left to learn about villages that had been vandalized and then excavated and stabilized in the early period of park development. That remained the conventional wisdom for years. But things gradually changed in part because excavation became so costly. Research into museum collections was much more cost effective. Balcony House was only one of many sites in the Southwest that were reexamined and with quite interesting results. With the water damage at Cliff Palace, it was not hard to convince granting institutions that the architecture, structural wood, rock art, plaster, and inscriptions of Cliff Palace deserved a serious reexamination. The architecture was particularly interesting, with the layout and function of a few rooms intriguing.

Several types of secular rooms were identified: living rooms (with hearths), granaries (for food), storage rooms (for non-food storage, with no evidence of a sealed doorway) and mealing rooms (with bins for grinding corn), along with open, unroofed areas, and miscellaneous structures such as terraces. Kivas were classified separately even though the hearths and heavy smoke blackening of walls suggests that they may have been used for habitation as well as ceremonial purposes. Rooms of various functions cluster into room suites, the living space of a household. Then these suites of rooms cluster into courtyard complexes which include one or more room suites associated with a kiva. Based on the number of room suites Cliff Palace had a permanent population of 25 households.

Just as Fewkes was concerned about the low room-to-kiva ratio found in Cliff Palace, so are modern researchers. Long House on Wetherill Mesa, the other large alcove village in Mesa Verde, has a similar low ratio. These two villages may have had special functions with the permanent residents using just a portion of the village. During special ceremonies, the village would have been used by a much larger population. Kivas then would have been used as sleeping quarters, a hypothesis based on the fact that there are a number of kivas without associated storage and living rooms, and areas in the site with unusual rooms such as those of the Speaker Chief's complex and two very large rooms with no hearths. Attributes such as size and plaster varied widely in the two courtyard complexes studied in detail, those damaged by water in 1995-96. All living rooms were on the ground floor and rooms of all types were smaller in one courtyard complex than the other. Doorway attributes bear a complex relationship with room function, probably because the function of rooms often changed over time. One courtyard complex contained from two to five room suites or households through time, with construction from 1260 to 1278. The other courtyard complex was constructed from 1268 to 1272 and evolved from one suite to two suites, or households. In both of these courtyards the room walls outlining the open courtyard were plastered and decorated.

Cliff Palace, like so many other cliff dwellings, has two discrete areas. And like many of the other sites, the physical division actually does not divide the village in half. One side of the dividing line contains many more rooms and kivas than the other. The dividing wall in Cliff Palace extends from the back of the alcove north of Room 62 to the north wall of Room 58. One of Fewkes' atypical kivas is on each side of the line and one large featureless room is on either side of the line. Recently dated wood places construction of these atypical kivas at 1278 and 1280. This is consistent with what has been found at Spruce Tree House and Balcony House where tree ring dates place construction of walls that restrict access from one part of the village to another in the late 1270s. The atypical kivas and the large featureless rooms are not found in Balcony House or Spruce Tree House but they may be comparable in function to the big rooms on either side of the large plazas at Long House and Fire Temple.

Cliff Palace also contains the unique area known as Speaker Chief's complex and Kiva Q. The outer layer of plaster on the lower walls of Kiva Q varies, with the north half of the kiva wall a slightly different color than the south half. Physical and visual divisions are being interpreted by researchers as representing a social division. Ethnographically, many Pueblo groups are known to be organized into two groups, or moieties. These social groups are not always based on kinship and are not spatially grouped in the physical layout of the modern villages. The Speaker Chief's complex is earlier than the dual division and was the focal point in the village by at least 1264. This conclusion is based primarily on a tree ring date from a room that is an addition to the main Speaker Chief's complex.

Conclusion

Cliff Palace, the largest village on the Mesa Verde, was built on a different scale than any other cliff dwelling in Mesa Verde National Park. As it presently exists, Cliff Palace dates from 1268 to 1280. This village contains the usual kivas, living rooms, storage rooms, and mealing rooms. Like many other cliff dwellings, a wall divides the village into two areas. But there is also a complex of rooms associated with a walled open area, Speaker Chief's complex. There is nothing comparable to Speaker Chief's complex and Kiva Q at other cliff dwellings. Possibly even more interesting and again unique to Cliff Palace, there is on either side of the dividing wall an atypical kiva and a very large room. Fewkes made note of these special areas and they still intrigue us a century later. Cliff Palace seems to be special. The park visitors certainly think so, based on its size and beauty. Archaeologists think so based on the layout and the special architectural features found in the village.

BALCONY HOUSE AND THE NUSBAUMS

Wednesday, January 4, 1995: I am working on my Balcony House report, trying to find original copies of Jesse Nusbaum's letters to Hewett. Then I remember a box of Nusbaum papers and photographs his step-daughter brought to the park in June 1993. I had seen some of the slides and papers but have no idea what else is in the box. The "stuff" is brought out from storage and the first thing I come across is a daily log on the Balcony House excavation of 1910 – a small notebook with handwritten entries. I first assume it is Nusbaum's notebook. But as I transcribe the contents, I see that the author refers to "Jess." It becomes obvious that it is his father's notebook when he refers to a letter from Agnes, his wife. In the notebook there is much about the horrible weather. He gets lost in a snow-storm trying to take a shortcut back to camp. This 59-year-old contractor and brickyard owner from Greeley is not enjoying his days on Mesa Verde.

Introduction

Balcony House is a great site. It has courtyards without kivas, tunnels, a huge retaining wall; and it is the only cliff dwelling that was excavated and stabilized by a future Mesa Verde National Park superintendent. Balcony House is located in quite a dramatic setting, on a ledge between the top of the mesa and the top of the talus. It is built in a small alcove that is part of this ledge within the upper Cliff House sandstone, not at the top of the talus; this is not unique to Balcony House but it is probably the largest cliff dwelling with this type of setting in the park. It is also unusual in that it faces somewhat north of due east, making it nice in the summer, sunny

Balcony House in 1892, Kiva Plaza.

and warm in the morning and cool and shady in the afternoon, but cold in the winter with almost no sunshine penetrating the alcove. There is a good spring in the site and another at the top of the talus 40 feet below.

Balcony House was constructed in the 13th century out of sandstone blocks that vary from finely finished stones pecked to shape to crudely shaped and hurriedly set stones. A beautiful balcony graces the front of a two-story complex of rooms. Balconies are not unique to Balcony House but this is by far the best preserved example of such a feature. The site consists of approximately 30 rooms and two kivas. In the foreground is a deep, wide canyon and in the background the horizon is interrupted by the peaks of the La Plata Mountains. There are other cliff dwellings across the canyon and also just up-canyon from Balcony House. Known for its 30-foot entrance ladder, knee-bruising tunnel and steep exit trail, Balcony House is a "must" visit for all adventurous park visitors.

In 1987, when I arrived at Mesa Verde, there was limited information on Balcony House. It consisted of Nordenskiöld's reference to the site in his early publication, some historic photos taken at the time of excavation, a plan map dating to 1910, three letters written during the excavation of the site, and 14 tree ring dates (of which six were cutting dates ranging from 1242 to 1278).

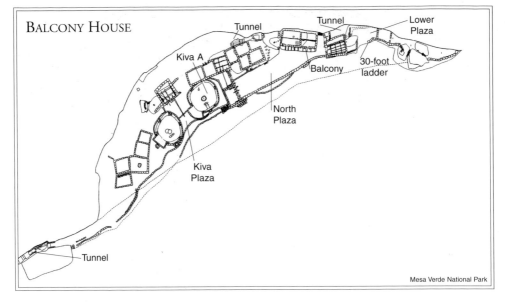

BALCONY HOUSE

Tunnel · Tunnel · Lower Plaza

Kiva A · Balcony · 30-foot ladder

North Plaza

Kiva Plaza

Tunnel

Mesa Verde National Park

Nordenskiöld and the Nusbaums

Balcony House is located in Soda Canyon, one of the main drainages of Mesa Verde (and a main access point for early explorers), so it is not surprising that this village was entered and reported on before such sites as Cliff Palace and Spruce Tree House. It was entered by at least 1884 and possibly earlier. "1884 S E Osborn March 22" is the earliest inscription with a date in the site. "W.H. Hayes 1884" is found in one of the balcony rooms. This may have been the same date as Osborn or, since Hayes was local, at some other time that year. Al Wetherill, who named the site, came through in 1885. Nordenskiöld mentioned Balcony House in his 1893 publication and there are some great pictures of the site as it looked in 1891, including the balcony and entrance tunnel. He commented on the nicely built walls of the rooms associated with the balcony.

With $1,000 to spend on a project in the new national park, the Colorado Cliff Dwellings Association proposed that Balcony House be excavated and stabilized. They turned to Edgar Hewett, of the Archaeological Institute of America, to head it up. Fewkes, who up to that time had done all the excavation and stabilization in the park, welcomed the help this would give in establishing Mesa Verde as a destination park.

Hewett selected Jesse Nusbaum to supervise the field operations. Nusbaum had worked for Hewett since 1907 when he was sent to Mesa Verde as a photographer on a student survey crew. He returned to the mesa in 1908. Then in 1909 he worked for Hewett restoring Santa Fe's Palace of the Governors, and the next summer assisted with excavation of Tyuonyi in what is now Bandelier National Monument.

I have never figured out why Hewett selected Nusbaum for the project at Balcony House. The young man was definitely one of his up-and-com-

Balcony House, Kiva Plaza in 1910. Metal is being prepared for use in this site. Jesse Nusbaum is shown on the left.

ing employees but it was a risk to put a 23-year-old with little experience and very limited archaeological training in charge. After all, the only other person who had worked in the park, Jesse Fewkes, was an experienced ethnographer/archaeologist with years of field work to his credit. Hewett was also in his prime (45 years old) but he made only one quick trip to Balcony House at the start of the project and another at the end. Otherwise he left Nusbaum on his own – no phones, no roads, no easy way to get help. There was a Western Union office in Mancos, and The Denver and Rio Grande Railroad linked Mancos and Durango to the outside world, but all were many miles from Balcony House.

Travel to the mesa was by horseback. Jack Adams, another employee of the Archaeological Institute of America, accompanied Nusbaum from Santa Fe, and Nusbaum was smart enough to hire someone with construction experience, his father, E.M. Nusbaum. A fellow named Tommy Gibbon also came from Greeley with his father. Other crew members were hired locally. At least one of these, Clint Scharf, had worked for Fewkes. The crew seems to have numbered from eight to 10, including a cook and a packer for water. Charles Kelly, a packer from Mancos, got the crew and equipment to and from the park.

On October 12, 1910, they began work on the site. It turned out to be

**Balcony House, 1910. Crew repairing Kiva A.
E.M. Nusbaum is standing in the background.**

a wet, cold fall with snow and freezing conditions for several days at a time. The site was in terrible condition. Two episodes of alcove roof collapse had left the southern portion of the site covered with slabs of sandstone and the retaining wall crushed and sliding down-canyon. Also, the spring in the back of the alcove in this portion of the site had, through the years, saturated the stones and mortar at the base of walls, leaving them in very unstable condition.

First the crew removed roof fall. Then they tackled the problem of the unsupported walls. Someone came up with the idea of using angle iron and turnbuckles to hold the walls in place while their bases were rebuilt. Nusbaum was a little nervous about this since Fewkes had not found it necessary to use such modern and very visible materials on a prehistoric site. But Park Superintendent Hans Randolph, Hewett, and Fewkes apparently went along with the technique. The next problem was to get material to the site as well as to get it paid for. During the entire four-week period of excavation and stabilization, October 12 to November 4, Nusbaum's constant worry was that he would not be able to complete the work with the budget he had been given.

He was slowed down by weather. Crew members, including his father, got sick. Materials had to be brought in from the railhead in Mancos by horse and wagon. Randolph went to bat for Nusbaum and got permission from the Department of Interior to make $500 budgeted for Fewkes available to Nusbaum. The project was completed at a cost of $1,514.12. The kiva walls were rebuilt – one collapsed in the process and had to be built again. The crew left November 4. Nusbaum and Adams drafted a plan map of the site while waiting for Hewett to give them the "okay" to leave. Hewett showed up days later, November 12, much later than expected and after dark, and then left early the next morning. On November 19, Nusbaum and Adams left in the middle of a snowstorm. What an experience!

During the Balcony House project Jesse Nusbaum was overwhelmed with the massive work load and the limited time and budget. He was convinced that the damage done by early visitors and collectors had compromised the site's scientific value. And he, like all these early archaeologists, was more interested in artifacts – whole artifacts – than architecture. It was frustrating to him that there were very few museum-quality objects recovered during his work at the site. He, of course, also had no tree ring dates so the construction dates were impossible to establish, except for older/younger based on wall abutments.

Years later Nusbaum returned to the park as superintendent, serving a total of 17 years over the span of two and a half decades. But he never really returned to Balcony House. He showed no scientific interest in the site through all those years. He didn't mention a site report and took no later photographs. As a manager/administrator, he devoted his energy to financing and building the park's infrastructure – roads, housing, administrative/museum complex – and excavating cliff dwellings with more promise for recovering museum quality objects for his new museum.

Soon after Nusbaum rode away from Balcony House that November day in 1910, there were concerns from the superintendent about the kivas the wall stones were constantly saturated with water, creating a risk of collapse. But nothing was done to solve the problem until 1939 when funding became available through New Deal legislation. Controlling water in Balcony House was one of many projects tackled by the Works Progress Administration. The problem was addressed by capturing the spring water in a trench in the back of Kiva Plaza, then running it through a subsurface pipe out to the front of the alcove. The system was upgraded in 1958, and by the time I showed up in the park, Balcony House was a dry alcove in very stable condition. In the early 1980s there was some discussion about removing the angle iron and turnbuckles, but when tension on one of the turnbuckles was relaxed and the wall moved slightly, all thought of removal was shelved. My stabilization philosophy was and remains "if something is working fine, leave it alone." The angle iron is unsightly but if the reason for its use is explained to the public, it just becomes another part of the site's very interesting history.

My Balcony House: Recent Research

When I arrived in the park, Balcony House was a stable, visually dramatic site but with almost no information that would be of interest to an archaeologist or someone charged with its preservation. In 1987 this site was the most poorly understood of the major cliff dwellings. Fewkes had published reports, short as they were, on Spruce Tree House and Cliff Palace, and the reports on the Wetherill sites of Long House and Mug House had been published fairly recently. Nordenskiöld's and Nusbaum's work in Step House was published. That left Balcony House.

So in 1988 I selected Balcony House as my special project, a way to maintain my interest in research and archaeology. My goal was to publish the material available within the park on Balcony House, and to add to that knowledge by reexamining the architecture, sampling all the wood in the site for dating, remapping the site, examining the Nusbaum papers at the National Anthropological Archives in Washington, D.C., and the Hewett papers and Nusbaum photographs in the archives of the Museum of New Mexico in Santa Fe. There was no funding in the stabilization budget for such research, so funding was dependent on grants from the Mesa Verde Museum Association, a National Park Service employee development grant, and Colorado state preservation grants. When I started, I had no idea the project would extend through virtually my whole career in the park, to December 2001 when I received my copy of the published report.

In 1988, park files contained copies of three letters Nusbaum wrote to Hewett during excavation, and some great photographs he took before, during and after excavation. Nusbaum's wife had written in a National Park Service publication that she had a copy of her husband's report on Balcony House – interesting in that he had never mentioned such a report. She had recently died and donated her husband's papers to the National Anthropological Archives in Washington, D.C., a part of the Smithsonian. One of the defining moments of my career came when I uncovered his field notes among his papers in the archives in Washington, D.C. That is when I really began my career-long love affair with Balcony House. An even more exciting moment came in 1995 when I found the diary kept by Nusbaum's father during the excavation. This totally unexpected treasure was great fun to read and transcribe, and gave a very personal view of a major park project.

What did the written and photographic records, tree ring dates, and reexamination of the physical attributes of the site tell us about Balcony House? In a nutshell, they established the 13th century construction history along with the access modifications made in the 1270s. The 20th century modifications made by the National Park Service were identified and the prehistoric and historic trails to and from the site were determined.

The Village

Nothing about the construction techniques used in Balcony House stands out as different. Some of the walls are beautifully built of shaped sandstone blocks. The walls of the rooms with the balcony extending across their front are some of the most beautiful in Mesa Verde. But there are other walls of no special note. The typical raised rectangular and square doorways are found throughout the site. One room has a painted dado with the fairly typical clusters of three triangles painted on the plaster and extending above the dado. It is the layout of the rooms, kivas, and tunnels that makes Balcony House unique. Research led to a complete reevaluation of movement into, through and out of Balcony House. I will present the results of this research as my understanding of the village evolved, by starting with 20th century Balcony House and working backward through time, ending with early 13th century Balcony House.

Late 20th century Balcony House: (bold type denotes park service structures in place to facilitate access by the public): Today, as it was when I arrived in the park, visitors begin their tour of Balcony House in the **parking lot**, wait for a **park service guide**, descend a series of stone and then **metal steps** to an **asphalt** trail, move south by a spring and then arrive at a **platform** on which is set a **30-foot ladder**. Visitors ascend the **ladder**, enter Lower Plaza, go through a tunnel and then up a **short ladder** to arrive in North Plaza where the namesake balcony is located. From North Plaza a **short ladder** and a few stone steps lead to another tunnel at the back of the alcove and into Kiva Plaza where two kivas are the most prominent features. Visitors then crawl through the tunnel at the south end of the village and ascend a very **steep series of ladders and steps** to arrive back in the parking lot. The park service access features were modifications made at various times between 1911 and 1950.

Early 20th century Balcony House: The Balcony House of the early 20th century was quite different. Up to and through the period of excavation in 1910, visitors to the site came from the mesa top above the site or from the bottom of Soda Canyon. Those coming up from the canyon had to scramble up a series of vertical cliffs to arrive at the top of the talus slope just below the ledge on which Balcony House is located. Those who were on the top of the mesa probably took a prehistoric trail north of the village down to the talus, then walked on a dirt trail at the top of the talus slope to again arrive just below Balcony House. The ruin was then entered via a ladder set just below Kiva Plaza. The site would have consisted of piles of rubble prior to excavation in 1910. The alcove roof had collapsed on two separate occasions between the 13th and 20th centuries, leading to the collapse of the east walls of the kivas and all evidence of the retaining wall for Kiva Plaza. The tunnel at the south end of Balcony House, the balcony, and much of the balustrade in North Plaza were in good condition. Visitors to the site

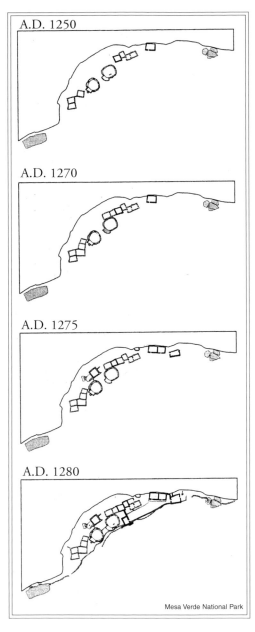

A.D. 1250

A.D. 1270

A.D. 1275

A.D. 1280

Mesa Verde National Park

Construction history of Balcony House A.D. 1250-1280. Plan view, room and kiva construction through time in the alcove. The dark lines delineate rooms that have been dated by tree-ring samples. Lighter lines delineate rooms with the construction period determined by wall abutments and other interpretations.

would have exited the ruin in the same manner as they entered.

Late 13th century Balcony House: This is the Balcony House Nusbaum uncovered. His field notes describe briefly the various rooms and features of Balcony House but there is no discussion of the overall layout of the village. The recent dating of the structural wood in the village really made the uniqueness of this 1270s village apparent. It could have been accessed either from the mesa top or the bottom of Soda Canyon. To my knowledge there is no prehistoric toehold trail in the cliffs below the site but with a good scramble this route is possible. From the mesa top to the top of the talus there are toehold trails both north and south of the village leading down to the top of the talus slope. To get up to the ledge on which Balcony House is located, it would have been necessary to ascend a 30-foot vertical cliff. There is no evidence of where this access was. There is an archaeological site at the south end of the ledge which consists of a fairly massive retaining wall and a former structure (now collapsed) which was either a tower or room block. High above the rubble mound is a petroglyph of a hand. Access to Balcony House probably first meant access through these structures. There are no depressions in the cliff face below these structures so a ladder or rope would have been necessary. Once on the ledge there is no problem walking north to the tunnel just south of the village (which in the

20th century is the exit tunnel). The tunnel leads to Kiva Plaza, where the two kivas would have been roofed. The two-story room between the kivas would be in place as would the rooms both north and south of the kivas.

A massive wall was built sometime during the 1270s to separate Kiva and North plazas. Access to North Plaza was via a wood platform and tunnel at the very back of the alcove. North Plaza would contain several balconies with the most impressive on the east wall of two rooms built side by side and each of two stories in height. To move even farther north through the village, a hatchway and another tunnel would lead into Lower Plaza with its crude walls built over, under and around a group of detached boulders. The real surprise of Balcony House is that all of these features controlling access from one part of the site to another lead, finally, to a part of the site with the least interest architecturally. There really is nothing to see at this very north end of the village.

I have speculated endlessly on the purpose of all the tunnels and hatchways and wondered what was so special about this north end of the site that made all these control features necessary. There is a great view down-canyon and it is the only portion of the village that receives direct sunshine on many days in winter. To exit the village it was necessary to return through all the tunnels and plazas.

Early 13th century Balcony House: This village was built at one end of a ledge that was 30 feet above the top of the talus. It was not an easy ledge to enter and its orientation slightly north of due east meant that on some days in winter there was no direct sunshine. But there was a great spring at the back of the alcove. Some construction had already occurred in the alcove, but it was either torn down or extensively modified in the 1240s. The village was entered from the south. Whether the retaining wall and room block at the very south end of the ledge were in place in the 1240s is not known. But the tunnel at the south end of the village would not have been constructed. The detached boulder that was incorporated into a tunnel in 1278 was initially just a detached boulder with a wide slot between it and the cliff face. It was possible to walk through this slot and enter the village. There would have been two kivas and two room blocks. The kivas were probably each in their own courtyard, each associated with a group of rooms for storage and habitation. One of the two-story rooms with a balcony on its east wall would be in place. The other two-story room with balcony and the room at the very north end of North Plaza would not have been built. They were built in 1275 and 1279, respectively so it would have been a very different village from 1270s Balcony House. None of the tunnels, hatchways, and platforms that control access from one portion of Balcony House to the next was built. This would have been a more typical two courtyard village with each kiva associated with a group of storage and habitation rooms.

It took me months of study to clarify in my mind all of the changes that occurred to Balcony House through time. It went from a typical two-courtyard village in the early 13th century, to a village dominated by features to control access through the village in the late 13th century. Hundreds of years later it went from a ruin that was looted and finally excavated and stabilized in the early 20th century to a park service exhibit that was modified to most efficiently move people through the exhibit in the late 20th century.

Although the motivations which led the park service to make the changes they did in the 20th century were never explicitly stated, there is little question that they were made to improve the visitor experience – increase safety, improve flow – and make the exhibit available to as many visitors as possible within a specified amount of time. These changes made an understanding of 13th century Balcony House almost impossible since many of the restrictions which made the village unique were removed. In their defense, no one in the park service had any idea these changes would so materially modify an understanding of the village.

THE LOCATION OF BALCONY HOUSE ON A HARD TO ACCESS LEDGE MAY SEEM DEFENSIVE BUT THE RESTRICTIONS THAT ARE WITHIN THE SITE SEEM TO BE DIFFERENT.
THEY REMIND ME MORE OF SITUATIONS WHERE MOVEMENT THROUGH SPACES BECOMES INCREASINGLY SECRET...

The motivations behind the numerous restrictions built into a fairly typical 1240s village in the 1270s are unknown. There is no question that movement through the village was intentionally and increasingly controlled through the 1270s. Space became more private and restricted as one moved north through the village. The location of Balcony House on a hard to access ledge may seem defensive but the restrictions that are within the site seem to be different. They remind me more of situations where movement through spaces becomes increasingly secret, limited to fewer and fewer individuals. It appears as if the concepts of public and private space became much more complex in the late 13th century. This was right before the migration that left Mesa Verde empty of farmers for the first time in 700 years and left the whole Northern San Juan area devoid of farmers for the first time in a thousand years.

Conclusion

Balcony House is a 13th century village and a 20th century travel destination. It began in the 13th century as a fairly typical two-courtyard village – two kivas with associated rooms, courtyards, and springs. In the 1270s the village was completely reorganized. Access into the site and between the three areas of the site was intentionally restricted. Soon thereafter the village occupants left their homes and the whole area and over time the site became a ruin. Then in the 20th century Balcony House was selected as one of the very few cliff dwellings to be excavated and stabilized so that it could be opened to the public. The need to efficiently move people through the pre-historic village required that many of the restrictive features be modified or removed. So, a small village that was inhabited for several generations and designed to restrict human movement was redesigned seven centuries later to function as an interpretive display for a large number of people.

Balcony House really is a must-see for the public. People actually walk through this site, not just up to it. They can see the shaped stones, the original mortar and plasters, and intact room roofs. They can bonk their heads against the balcony as well as crawl through a tunnel and climb a 30-foot ladder. All in all, it is a very memorable experience. Everyone may want to see Cliff Palace, but it is Balcony House that visitors remember.

LONG HOUSE: RAYMOND'S RUIN

November 13, 1998, Shiprock, New Mexico: Patti Bell and I are interviewing Raymond Begay, retired stabilization crew chief. He was on the crew from 1958 to 1998 and his first major project was the stabilization of Long House, "Raymond's ruin." During the interview I ask him about a burial in Long House.

Kathy: "Raymond, remember telling me about a burial up by the spring in Long House?"

Raymond: "Some guys were working up in Long House and they found a skeleton. They said 'over here, over here.' They'd always call, '*chindi*, *chindi*' when they found a skeleton. To the Navajos the '*chindi*' is a ghost. So they found a skeleton, these kids [archaeologists], and they said, '*chindi*, *chindi*.' Everybody ran over there. Way behind the dirt, they found a turkey and baby. I think it was a little baby. You know how they weave the turkey feathers, small kind of feathers. Inside to keep them warm. They make something to pad the babies, and the babies sleep in it in the winter time. The baby's in there and about this tall. The baby's laid there, and the turkey's sitting right up, just like a live turkey sits up. Right there with the baby. The skin was dry, all dry against the bones. Some of the feathers were still on. The baby's skin, too. The skin was all dry. The baby was a mummy, too. Its head was small. Just a little baby."

Long House in 1952, before excavation, and before fire in 2000 stripped the surrounding area of vegetation.

Introduction

Raymond Begay did his apprenticeship on this village from 1959 to 1962. Not a bad place to spend four years. While the archaeologists were recording room features and mapping the site, Raymond was mixing mortar, and shaping and setting stones.

Long House is located in a stunningly beautiful setting, best seen from the overlook on the Badger House Community Loop Road. I've read that our sense of beauty has a lot to do with symmetry, so maybe that is why Long House never fails to impress the observer. The alcove is large, both broad and high, and the village is perfectly situated within the space to emphasize the symmetry. A large plaza is in front, with clusters of kivas and rooms behind and to the east and west. The high walls of rooms add interest, as do the walls visible on several high ledges within the alcove. The alcove is located at the head of a short side canyon on Wetherill Mesa with a dramatic view of Rock Canyon to the south. Since the alcove is oriented to the south, it enjoys relatively long hours of sunshine on cold clear winter days and in summer with the sun high in the sky, the village is bathed in shade. There is an active, dependable spring in the back of the alcove. It is no surprise that this cliff dwelling is the featured attraction of Wetherill Mesa.

20th Century History

Nordenskiöld spent a month in Long House, from July 14 to August 14, 1891. He mentioned that the site was in bad shape, and surprisingly few of the objects illustrated in his 1893 publication are from this site where he spent the majority of his time. Seventy years later Cattanach and Lancaster also commented that the site was in bad shape. Long House was completely excavated as part of the Wetherill Mesa Project from 1958 to 1962, a time when tree ring dating, stratigraphy, pottery analysis, and floral and faunal research were all accepted and expected operating procedures. A seasoned park service archaeologist, George Cattanach, Jr., was put in charge of the project and Al Lancaster was his right-hand man supervising both the excavation and stabilization. The published report is a clear and thorough discussion of the results. Recently, the tree ring data from the site was reassessed, with old samples reexamined and new ones removed from previously unsampled in situ wood. It is apparent that occupation at Long House was protracted and complex. Probably many of the bigger alcoves were occupied over a long period of time but only Long House and Mug House have benefited from modern, research-oriented excavation and then publication of the results of this research.

Prehistory

The site's history can be broken into several phases. The Long House alcove was part of Mesa Verde's first occupation in the 7th century. A pithouse dating to 648 was uncovered during the Wetherill Mesa Project on the east side of the alcove underneath several 13th century rooms. Tree ring dates suggest it was repaired in 655 and again in 667 and sometime after that was destroyed by fire. Then there is a long period with little firm evidence of construction in the alcove. Early versions of later kivas may date back this early but there is no hard evidence.

There was a period of major construction between 1145 and 1205, no construction or repairs from 1206 to 1245, then a period of construction and repair between 1246 and 1259. Around 1260 there is evidence of a major disaster, including the movement of a boulder resulting in the loss of walls, fire in many rooms and kivas, and death without burial of several people. Many of the rooms and kivas were then rebuilt, reoccupied from 1261 to 1274 with minor changes up to 1279. As is being found at many cliff dwellings, this last occupation appears the most defensive, based on the construction of loopholes (lookout holes), tower, and massive wall at the front of the site. The careful excavation and recent tree ring research has established that not all of the 21 kivas that are now visible were in use at the same time. Rooms and kivas were built, used, filled in and new ones built close by or even on top of the previous construction.

One of the interesting aspects of Long House is the centrally located space variously called a plaza or great kiva. The 56-foot by 34-foot area, which was never roofed, was uncovered during excavation in the 1960s. There had been no hint of it in Nordenskiöld's day, when it was covered by several feet of debris from collapsed roofs and walls. A similar 42-foot by 23-foot plaza on Chapin Mesa in Fire Temple is in much better condition

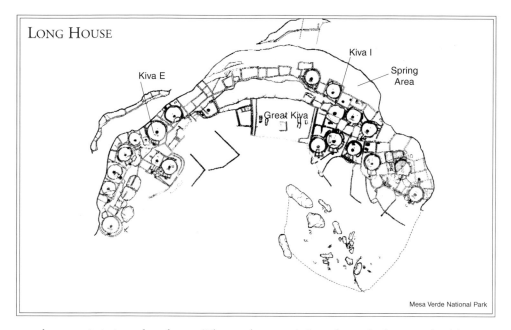

LONG HOUSE

Kiva E

Kiva I

Spring Area

Great Kiva

Mesa Verde National Park

because it is in a dry alcove. There, the remaining plaster is decorated with some of the most interesting pictographs in the park and the flanking massive, high structures which define the plaza's east and west sides are still standing. At Long House, however, whatever plaster may have existed is now long gone and the rooms that define the space to the east and west are, unfortunately, fragments of their former selves.

At Long House a seep along the bedrock which forms the back of the plaza has led to serious preservation problems – salts, vegetation, masonry deterioration, and mortar loss. Unfortunately there are no tree ring dates from this plaza and so few artifacts that its actual function is unknown. The description of it as a plaza or great kiva is based exclusively on architecture and location within the site. "No greater controversy has arisen from the excavation of Long House than over the proper term for the central plaza or court Lancaster and I prefer to call a great kiva," Cattanach wrote in his 1980 report. He placed construction of this feature in the 1240s.

One of the great resources of the Long House alcove, and undoubtedly one of the reasons why Mesa Verdeans in the 7th and 13th centuries valued this alcove, is the very reliable spring in the back of the upper ledge. At some time in the past, several water collecting basins were ground into the bedrock floor of the ledge, a few of them quite deep. There are approximately 20 large basins and many more small ones. Some even have feeder grooves that direct the flow of water to a particular basin or series of basins. I don't know of any other wet alcove with such a modification.

The two large cliff dwellings that have been carefully excavated with concern for stratigraphy and provenience are Long House and Mug House. Their layouts are quite different. The west-facing Mug House alcove is filled to overflowing with construction – rooms and courtyards added with no preplanning. The village is divided by a large wall that separates the north and south portions of the village. There are four kivas (five if the *kihu*, a rectangular structure that looks much like a kiva, is counted) to the north of the wall and three to the south. Another kiva is out in front, as if it straddles the two halves. In contrast, Long House was constructed in a huge south-facing alcove that dominates the landscape. The village is just one part of the greater whole. There is no feeling that the village is falling out of the alcove as at Mug House. While there is no obvious preplanning at Long House, the symmetry is so incredible that it is hard to believe there wasn't at least some vision of what layout was desired. The village is divided by the central great kiva (or if one prefers, plaza) and above this the spring area with several rooms and two kivas. To the west there are 10 kivas and to the east nine. Tree ring dates make it clear that not all of these kivas and rooms were occupied at the same time but the east-west division was constant. Also, many of these kivas are associated with few to no rooms, suggesting that Long House functioned much as Cliff Palace: a gathering place for villagers from the surrounding communities.

Because both Long House and Mug House were completely excavated using modern techniques, a comparison of architecture and artifacts can be made (see chart). While fewer broken pottery pieces were found at Mug House, significantly more complete or restorable vessels were unearthed there. Both sites contained a similar number of metates but Mug House had many more manos. Two objects, carved sticks (prayer sticks) and finely made hoes (*tchamahias*), are considered of ceremonial/religious significance. Only Long House contained carved sticks, in fact 15 if those collected by Nordenskiöld are included. The number of hoes collected was similar at each site, as was the number of burials. In both cases most burials were found in the deposits in front of the site but some were found within the village. Almost no non-local objects were found in the excavated deposits of either village.

A lot of things other than Pueblo cultural behavior can account for these differences, such as the amount of disturbance and uncontrolled collection

EXCAVATION COMPARISONS

	Kiva/ kihu	Rooms	Towers	Mealing	Sherds	Whole Pots	Metates	Manos	Carved Sticks	Tchamhia	Burials
LONG HOUSE:	21	94	1	4	63,000	295	96	338	8(15)	17	40
MUG HOUSE:	9	80	2	2	50,000	424	105	492	0	14	46

WAS THERE VIOLENCE?

The question of violence and cannibalism is a hot topic in the Southwest. One physical anthropologist has interpreted the burial context and condition of bones at four sites within Mesa Verde National Park as suggestive of violence and, in one case, possible cannibalism. Two others who looked at the same remains disagree.

At Long House the human remains found in Kiva M, and possibly also remains from Kivas K and O, suggest violence. In this case a total of three individuals are involved. Two sites in the Far View area of Chapin Mesa that have now been backfilled had remains that suggested a violent death, one body from one site and six from another. The bones of one body from Coyote Village in the Far View area have physical attributes that suggest cannibalism to physical anthropologist Christy Turner: breakage, cut marks, anvil abrasions and possible burning. However, another team of physical anthropologists who studied the same remains did not find evidence of cannibalism. It must be emphasized that violence (10) and cannibalism (1, disputed by some) are associated with only a very small percentage of the human remains (over 200) found in Mesa Verde archaeological sites – remains that represent 800 years of occupation.

The National Park Service has followed the advice of its Native American consultation group and at present does not allow examination of these human remains by professional physical anthropologists. Although I sympathize with the Native American consultants and realize that they find this a painful topic, I sincerely believe that ignoring evidence and removing it from study, is not the appropriate response. Violence and cannibalism, like any other human activity, must be studied and understood. The question of "why?" must be addressed in an open forum. Only then will the activities that led to such actions be put in their appropriate context and become more than just a sensational theory.

---

prior to excavation, but they just might signify a real difference in what was going on at the two villages. It is this type of data that archaeologists use to come up with theories about Pueblo social organization. Some have concluded that Long House and also Cliff Palace were special purpose sites. Other archaeologists are still waiting for more comparative data.

Stabilization

The Wetherill Mesa Project was designed to maximize the information that could be acquired from archaeological sites. So instead of the few weeks spent cleaning up a site such as Cliff Palace decades earlier, five years were spent in the field at Long House, 1958-1962. The downside of such complete research was that late construction had to be damaged in order to get to earlier deposits. Floor levels dating to the 1270s were removed to get to earlier floors dating to the 600s. As a result, we know a lot more about the history of Long House than Cliff Palace or Balcony House, but a much lower percentage of the site is original. Also, Long House was in particularly bad condition prior to excavation. Whether this was due to 19th century looting or original construction techniques is not known, but the result is a heavily stabilized site.

In the 1950s and '60s portland cement was a much-used mortar in stabilization and a lot was utilized in Long House. In this wet alcove, original site stones have deteriorated while the concrete mortar in which they were reset remains as hard and unyielding as the day it dried. When the concrete mortar cracks and becomes loose in joints, it is replaced with modern acrylic-modified earthen mortar, which demands much more frequent replacement than concrete mortars but is much better for the site stone.

During the Wetherill Mesa Project a copper lip was placed along the top of the alcove's dripline, right over the center of the site, which has definitely helped preserve the great kiva's front wall as well as what remains of the rooms to its east and west. However, during a heavy downpour as happened in 1987, torrential water cascading over the edge of the mesa has a devastating impact on the deposits in front of the site. These deposits are part of what must be preserved because they often contain burials as well as trash from the village. Stones were placed over these loose deposits in the 1960s to stabilize the area. In 1987 the stones washed out and had to be replaced.

Although the reliable spring in back of the upper ledge was undoubtedly a benefit for the village of Long House, the water is a nightmare for preservation. Nothing has been done to control and then move it out of the village. There is no obvious way to do so without drilling through bedrock from the upper ledge to the front of the site, and no one has considered that a good idea. So in my time when the preservation crew was in the site, they manually removed the water from the basins ground into the bedrock. When no one is there to remove the water, it seeps through the sandstone and saturates the bedrock along the north wall of the great kiva. A variety of vegetation grows in these wet areas and deposits of salt are also a problem. Interestingly, the 2000 fire on Wetherill Mesa changed the water flow pattern, moving it from the middle of the upper ledge to the east end.

To give Wetherill Mesa visitors a similar experience to their counterparts on Chapin Mesa, in 1961 one of the kivas in Long House was roofed like the covered kiva in Spruce Tree House. Unfortunately, Long House is not in a dry alcove as is Spruce Tree House, so the result has been a preservation disaster. The covered kiva stays damp all the time – even in winter it is like entering the tropics to drop into this kiva. The dirt mortars never dry out, the building stones lose their integrity through time and have to be replaced, and moss grows on all surfaces. A solar-operated fan was rigged up to at least reduce the humidity in the kiva, and it helped. It worked even better after an engineer pointed out that it was better to suck air out rather than blow outside air in. The system was installed every fall after the last visitors left and remained in place until the next visitor season – on Wetherill that is typically Memorial Day to Labor Day. The real solution to the problem would be to backfill the kiva (after all, there are many more on exhibit in Long House) or at least remove much of the roof so air can circulate more naturally.

At Long House, as with Balcony House and the early trail through Cliff Palace, original walls were at some point modified or removed to allow visitor movement through the site. At Long House there is a question about when this occurred. Even in Nordenskiöld's day there was a break in the parapet wall just west of the great kiva. Whether this was done in the 13th century or even before Nordenskiöld in the 19th century is impossible to establish. The park service uses this break as a part of its trail through the upper, back part of the village. Two ladders allow visitors to view the spring area at the very back of the alcove and then exit by walking over room walls. This is great for getting groups of people through Long House, but it is not good for a clear understanding of the original layout of the village. It is obvious that most of the larger villages were designed to restrict movement from

Mesa Verde National Park

Lon Ayers, 1990, removing tree ring sample from lintel in the backcountry.

one portion to the other with walls, placement of wall openings, and hatchways. Even in the large and remarkably open site of Long House, access to the upper ledge with its spring was controlled by the construction of rooms, parapet walls, and kivas surrounding the ledge.

Tree Ring Research

When I arrived in the park, I was surprised at how little wood in many of the major cliff dwellings had been sampled for tree ring dating. But I shouldn't have been. Many of these sites had been cleaned up before the development of this technique and this research was competing with all sorts of other research and preservation needs. But it was a research area that could rather easily be developed even on limited budgets – and perfect for a person like me who is fascinated with the evolution of villages through time. Also, battery-operated hand drills with small specialized bits – a vast improvement over one-inch bits on manually operated drills – had made the removal of hundreds of samples quick and efficient with very little

WOOD SAMPLING RESULTS

	# of Dates	Earliest Date	Latest Date	Clusters
Spruce Tree House	262	1124	1278	1230s, 1240s
Cliff Palace	69	1108	1275	1270s
Balcony House	154	1203	1279	1240s, 1270s
Square Tower House	182 (130 from two kivas)	1150	1282	1200s, 1260s, late 1270s
Oak Tree House	56	1165	1209	1190s, 1200s
Spring House	121	1195	1279	1200,1240s,1260-1279
20½ House	30	1211	1272	1240s, 1260s
Long House	838	630	1279	640s, 1250s, 1260s, 1270s
Step House	173	547	1240	610-625
Mug House	89	1011	1276	around 1260

impact on the original wood. The Laboratory of Tree-Ring Research at the University of Arizona under Jeff Dean agreed to send its staff to the park to do the sampling, covering salaries and travel. The park agreed to supply housing for the crew; and on the initial project, a grant from the Mesa Verde Museum Association covered the cost of analyzing each sample.

Balcony House was the first site selected for tree ring research, followed by Spruce Tree House, Square Tower House, Spring House and 20½ House which were all sampled by Tree Ring Lab staff; and Oak Tree House and Cliff Palace which were sampled by park service staff. Before all this research, the excavated sites on Wetherill Mesa were the best-dated sites in the park. Afterward, they were the poor cousins.

In the days of the Wetherill Mesa Project, juniper (the most commonly used wood for construction in Mesa Verde), was not datable. By the 1990s it was possible to date juniper and the master chronology for the area had been refined so in 2001 the old samples from Wetherill Mesa were reanalyzed to be comparable with the 1990s research. Also, a graduate student working at the Tree Ring Lab was interested in doing a comprehensive sampling of the wood in Long House as part of his dissertation research. So in 1999 the wood in Long House was re-sampled and in 2001 both of these projects – the reanalysis of the Wetherill Mesa samples and the dissertation research – were completed.

The Long House research shows what can be done when complete, modern excavation techniques are combined with a complete wood sampling strategy. Long House is now undoubtedly the best documented and the best-dated cliff dwellings in the Southwest. There are 838 dated wood samples (out of a total of 1136 samples) from the village and the sequence of construction and abandonment for Long House is based on this research. Kiva I at Long House is an excellent example of the value of intensive wood sampling in one structure. The distribution and clustering of 49 dated tree ring samples in Kiva I suggest it was built over three winters. The vent shaft and possibly lower walls were built in the winter of 1270-71, the upper walls in 1271-72, and the roof in 1272-73.

The wood in nine cliff dwellings has been studied in the last 20 years: five sites on Chapin Mesa (Balcony House, Cliff Palace, Spruce Tree House, Square Tower House and Oak Tree House), two sites on Long Mesa which is between Chapin and Wetherill mesas (Spring House and 20½ House), and three sites on Wetherill Mesa (Long House, Mug House and Step House). With Mug House and Step House the old samples were reanalyzed but no new samples were removed from the wood in the villages.

All of the dated cliff dwellings were built between the 1180s and 1280 with most construction between the 1230s and the 1270s. Oak Tree House has the earliest dated Pueblo III rooms with all construction dates falling between 1180 and 1210 and most in the 1190s. But a whole section of Oak Tree village lacks wood and on the basis of layout and architecture, is considered the latest construction in the village. In all other well-dated villages there was at least some construction into the 1270s.

All three of the well-excavated sites – Mug House, Step House, and Long House – have evidence of an occupation before construction of the cliff dwelling. Step House has six 7th century pithouses; Long House has one 7th century pithouse; and Mug House has enough dates in the 11th century to suggest a Pueblo II occupation. The rest of these villages have not benefited from modern and comprehensive excavation or have not been excavated at all. But all of them contain reused wood from trees that were cut down well before the room in which it is now located was built, based on wall abutments and the date of other wood in the room. This suggests that most of these villages obscured earlier rooms, pithouses, and kivas.

Conclusion

Long House produced many surprises in those heady days when the site was relinquishing its secrets layer by layer – from a great kiva similar to one Fewkes had excavated on Chapin Mesa in Fire Temple, to the burial of a small child wrapped in a feather blanket and resting next to the burial of a turkey. Recent research suggests that the occupants of the cliff dwelling suffered a major upheaval around 1260 but then rebuilt the site and lived there another 20 years. The number of kivas, the great kiva, and the number of carved sticks from the site suggest it was a special ceremonial site in the 13th century. In the 21st century it remains a special site, but as an interpretive exhibit. Long House offers visitors a breathtaking view of a huge alcove, a very symmetrical village, and kivas, rooms, and water collecting basins in this spectacular setting.

Myers Walker, Sally Cole

Digitized historic and recent photographs were used to recreate the appearance of a plaster panel in Kiva E in Long House by volunteer Myers Walker. This polychrome plaster panel suffers from flaking and detachment and is in part covered by a deposit of pack rat excrement.

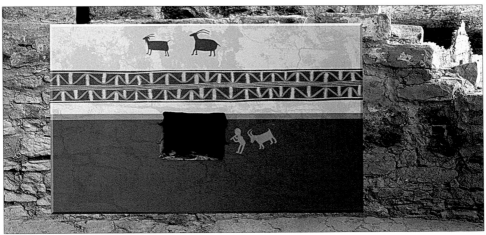

Myers Walker, Sally Cole

A digitized recreation of the panel showing what it would have looked like originally, based on the remaining evidence.

STEP HOUSE: STAIRS AND STARS

April 2001: A group of Hopi are in Step House. They look up at a series of black cross-like images and pinkish-white streaks on the ceiling of the alcove. They interpret these as *sootu*, the Milky Way.

Introduction

Step House generates very mixed emotions. Archaeologists love the site. It has, in fact, been excavated three times – the only site in the park with such a history. Nordenskiöld's comments are typical: insignificant appearance, exceedingly great interest. Visitors find the site disappointing. They don't often notice the stairs; the cliff dwelling is small and overwhelmed by the alcove itself; the pithouses are so completely rebuilt that anyone can see there is little original fabric; and the trail is long and hot in the summer. Those with a preservation background are intrigued and horrified by its recent history – one of the most distinctive plaster panels in the park was lost fairly recently; the reconstructed pithouse superstructure was crushed by a slab off the roof of the alcove soon after it was built; and bees and dust are a persistent problem.

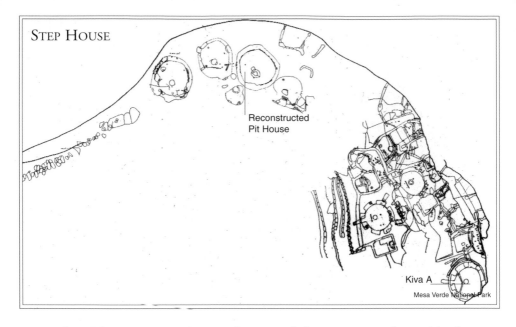

STEP HOUSE

Reconstructed
Pit House

Kiva A

Mesa Verde National Park

Step House is unique in several ways and deserves some of any visitor's time on Wetherill Mesa. The Step House alcove was occupied by early farmers in the 7th century. It was then unoccupied for several hundred years before it was reoccupied in the 13th century, when a relatively small cliff dwelling was built in this huge alcove. While four of the six early pit-houses were built near the center and lowest portion of the alcove, the cliff dwelling was built at the high, most northerly portion. Consequently, structures from both of these occupations can be viewed today.

Another unique attribute of Step House is the stairway. Sandstone slabs have been placed along the cliff face at the south end of the alcove in such a way as to form a stairway which extends from the floor of the alcove almost to the mesa top. There is still a band of vertical cliff at the very top of the mesa which must be scrambled over or scaled by ladder. The staircase allows easy access into the alcove, wide steps that even 20th century individuals with a fear of heights could use – not the typical toe- and hand-hold trails into many cliff dwellings. When the stairway was built is not known. It could as easily date to the 7th century occupation as the later 13th century cliff dwelling occupation. Because it is an original feature of the site, it is not used for access into the alcove today but can be seen once in the site.

Archaeologists' added interest in Step House is due to its excavation history. It was here that some of the defining moments in the history of southwestern archaeology took place. This multi-component site with the two components mostly next to each other, not one on top of the other, is where the early struggles with the concept of stratigraphy, and "Basket Maker" vs. "Cliff Dweller" took place. Undoubtedly many of the cliff dwellings cover structures that date back to an earlier time period. In fact, at Long House an early pithouse was partially uncovered during excavation. But at Step House much of the early research was in deposits not obscured by later structures.

Of equal interest to archaeologists, the artifacts associated with these pithouses are different from those associated with the cliff dwelling. In 1891 Nordenskiöld only mentioned in passing the possible difference in age of certain materials, but by the time Nusbaum wrote about his 1926 excavations in the Step House alcove (1949), the distinction between Basketmaker and Pueblo was established. It was also known by then that Basketmaker was just an earlier version of the same Pueblo culture. The importance of stratigraphy to archaeologists – the superposition of materials through time – grew out of such work as that done at Step House.

History of Research

The first report on excavations in Step House was by Nordenskiöld, who was fascinated with the burials and associated artifacts he uncovered. Even at this early date (excavation in 1891, report in 1893), Nordenskiöld mentioned "previous excavations of a less thorough description." He uncovered eight burials from the area covered with trash, located between the cliff dwelling at the north end of the site and the stairway at the south end of the site.

Even more interesting, two feet deep, he found a bowl and ladle of very crude construction. In his section on pottery, Nordenskiöld speculated that these vessels might be older than the rest of the pottery he uncovered and were "perhaps the work of people who inhabited Step House cave before the erection of cliff villages." He did not work in the cliff dwelling and he did not dig deep enough to uncover any pithouses.

As the 20th century began, people interested in the Southwest and its early history were both creating the field of southwestern archaeology and expanding on and clarifying the disparate data accumulated by the early explorers and initial researchers. The importance of stratigraphy in isolating different time periods was slowly spreading from Europe to the Southwest. At the same time, researchers were forming a distinction between "Cliff Dweller" and "Basket Maker" and focusing on pottery to define different time periods. Nordenskiöld's work in Step House and Fewkes' excavations of Earth Lodge A in 1919 both pointed toward an early, pre-Cliff Dweller occupation of the mesa. While Fewkes was excavating in Mesa Verde, Nusbaum was caught up in this drive for an understanding of early farming development in the Southwest. In 1920 the Museum of the American Indian in New York sent him to Dupont Cave in Utah which contained deposits similar to what the Wetherills had termed "Basket Maker."

The Wetherills' collecting in Utah, after their explorations in Mesa Verde including Step House, established the initial distinction between the "Basket Makers" and the "Cliff Dwellers." At the western edge of the

Northern San Juan culture area they found evidence of farmers who used atlatls instead of bows and arrows, and baskets instead of pottery – obviously earlier than any Step House deposits. Nusbaum, among others, was intrigued by this pre-pottery and early pottery period. So when he returned to Mesa Verde as superintendent in 1921, it is not surprising that he turned to Step House for his first major research project. He was not only familiar with the Nordenskiöld publication's illustrations of potentially early pottery from Step House, but Nusbaum had a 10-year background in excavation and at least some realization of the importance of stratigraphy in establishing the span of time reflected in the deposits.

In 1925 Nusbaum began by training a crew in excavation techniques in the trash at the back of Spruce Tree House alcove. Then in early 1926 they moved on to Step House. Here he uncovered the lower walls and floors of three pithouses, an exterior firepit and what he interpreted as a possible pottery shrine.

In the introduction to his report, Nusbaum discussed the early history of excavation in the site, including collecting in the alcove by the Wetherills in 1890, the Wetherills with Nordenskiöld in 1891, and then the Wetherills again in 1892 when they were collecting for the Colorado Historical Society. A manuscript by Wetherill brother-in-law Charlie Mason on the 1892 collecting mentioned that cliff dweller material was found in the upper deposits, below which there was a layer of sterile material over burned building material associated with crude early basket-impressed pottery. Nusbaum dated this manuscript to 1917. Mason's manuscript and Nusbaum's discussion with John Wetherill in 1908 led Nusbaum to believe that the Wetherills did not realize the significance of stratigraphy and that neither they nor Nordenskiöld realized they had uncovered evidence of an earlier people in Step House. At least by 1949 when Nusbaum wrote his Step House report, he certainly realized that the lowest deposits were Basketmaker and in fact he had tree ring dates that gave the pithouses he excavated a definite construction date. The cutting dates gave a range from 593 to 626. Nusbaum excavated in the lowest portion of the alcove, the same area that Nordenskiöld tested. Both of these men avoided the cliff dwelling in the north end of the alcove.

During his excavations, Nusbaum could isolate areas that had been disturbed previously. Nordenskiöld had dug into the lower Basketmaker deposits in only one area, one he believed might hold evidence of a cremation. In fact Nusbaum discovered that Nordenskiöld had excavated down to slabs that were a portion of the wall of Nusbaum's Room A. Stratigraphically, during his excavations, Nusbaum found an upper lens of disturbed fill. Below that he found Pueblo III deposits. Then there was a layer of sterile fill that contained no cultural material. This was over material from the burned and collapsed roofs and walls of rooms, and finally the floors of three "rooms." Nusbaum, in fact, found the same sequence of lev-

View of flight of steps that are the south access to Step House. This photo is from a report by Jesse Nusbaum that was completed in 1949.

Rooms A, B and C in Step House, after excavation. This photo was taken by Jesse Nusbaum and included in his report that was completed in 1949.

els as had Mason in 1892. Two of the three structures Nusbaum excavated had firepits and four post holes in their floors, and the lower walls of all three were lined with upright, sandstone slabs.

We now call these structures Basketmaker III pithouses. Fairly common in Mesa Verde, they are found both on the mesa top and in alcoves and date to the Basketmaker III period, 500-700. In Mesa Verde all excavated pithouses date to the last half of this period.

Besides finding more than 2,000 sherds of crude fired and unfired pottery, Nusbaum found such things as 15 jars and bowls, 29 miniature pottery toys and effigies, two trough metates, eight one-hand manos, two projectile points, 11 sandals, a stone pendant, five bone awls, a skin bag, and evidence of corn, squash, and beans. Unfortunately none of these are illustrated in the publication. These objects with their associated structures made it clear that at Step House Nusbaum was not dealing with the earliest adaptation to farming as in Utah. In southeast Utah large slab-lined cists were associated with baskets and there was no evidence of pottery.

In the 1950s when the Wetherill Mesa Project was being planned, Step House was an obvious alcove to include in the interpretive plans for the mesa, with its two distinct occupations separated by 600 years. Robert

Nichols was in charge of the 1962 excavations, Al Lancaster the stabilization. The pueblo was in particularly bad shape, which was odd since the alcove was dry. Early rummaging through the site may have done some of the damage, but the fact that the walls of the village were built on cultural fill was probably the main culprit. Loose fill containing lots of dry, intact vegetal material attracts a significant number of rodents, and to this day they are a big problem in Step House. Even so, many corn kernels, bean seeds, and seeds of native plants have been found in the fill from this site. It also didn't help that many walls were built on and around detached boulders with their uneven surfaces.

The needs of interpretation and stabilization directed the course of work in 1962. Excavation uncovered another pithouse in the central portion of the site, making a total of four for that area. Then researchers uncovered two pithouses beneath the small pueblo at the north end of the site. The artifacts associated with these early pithouses included fragments of woven sandals and baskets, bone awls, corncobs, squash fragments, plain grey pottery sherds, and lots of evidence of the use of wild plants and animals, amaranth, Indian rice grass, deer, cottontail rabbits, as well as corncobs and kernels, seeds, and turkey bone. In the later 13th century pueblo, three kivas and 20 or so rooms (roofed areas) were excavated and stabilized for visitation. The exact number of rooms is difficult to establish because some of the rooms may have had multiple stories and several walled areas may have been roofed originally even though there was no evidence of that roofing at the time of excavation. Associated with the pueblo were typical PIII pottery, turkey and cottontail bones, lots of evidence of corn, bean, and squash remains, and lots of turkey droppings.

Although there has been a long history of research at Step House, publication of the results has not always been timely. Nordenskiöld did a good job with his 1893 publication. But Nusbaum didn't complete the report on his 1926 research until 23 years later, in 1949, and another 32 years passed before it was published in 1981. Nichols' research was in 1962, the report completed in 1972. It has yet to be published.

Stabilization

The stabilization history of Step House follows in the tradition of the publication history: fits and starts with lots of problems. The three pithouses excavated by Nusbaum were left to deteriorate after exposure until 1935, when loose fill was removed. Some work was also done on the unexcavated cliff dwelling in that year. But it was the pithouses that were the problem. The unstable walls and loose fill into which they were dug led to rapid deterioration through time both after 1926 and after 1935. So when it was decided to exhibit the pueblo and the three Nusbaum pithouses in the lower portion of the alcove, the pithouses were the big challenge. Also added to this, the Wetherill Mesa Project's advisory committee of southwestern scholars decided to reconstruct much of the walls and the roof of one of the pithouses. So over the original floor and lower walls, the park erected four upright posts, the four stringers between the posts, the wood forming the walls and roof, and the upright stone slabs at the base of the walls. A portion of the east wall was left open so visitors could see into the structure. Then instead of mud, the structure was covered with a tinted portland cement mortar. The details of the reconstruction were based on evidence from floor features but also on the remains of collapsed walls and roofs associated with other excavated pithouses in the park. Seventeen years after the reconstruction was completed, a slab detached from the alcove ceiling, crushing a portion of it. The damage was repaired and this re-reconstructed pithouse has been on exhibit in Step House for many years.

The crushed reconstructed pithouse was only one of many preservation problems in Step House. To preserve the outline of the other three pithouses, the walls had to be almost completely rebuilt. Much of the original floors with their features remain, but the lower walls are 1960s reconstruction. Rodents, particularly ground squirrels, have been a problem. Through the years a repellent, smoke bombs, mothballs, and live trapping were all tried, but the rodents persist.

Ground bees laying their eggs in holes they dig in dirt are also a problem. They seem to love to dig holes in the mortar of Kiva A, laying their eggs in early summer and then leaving. Initially these holes were filled with a mud mortar in the hope it would discourage the bees. It did, but only marginally. My final answer was to put flexible window screening over the areas of bee activity from May through July. Covering those areas the bees favored with plastic mesh definitely worked, but there was some movement into areas of the site that had not previously been disturbed. Basically, though, the technique was a success.

The most serious preservation problem in Step House was the deterioration of plaster in Kiva A. A series of very unusual images on the plaster began to deteriorate soon after excavation in 1962, but no direct intervention took place. Removal seemed inappropriate for a site on exhibit and reattachment of mud plasters was still experimental. Some plaster reattachment research was initiated in Mug House but no one in the park was trained in any plaster preservation techniques. The stabilization crew had always dealt with replacing deteriorating materials – mortars and stones – not with developing ways to preserve construction materials.

When much of this plaster panel collapsed in 1988, it focused attention on the need to do something about deteriorating plaster in the park. It was too late for the Step House panel. Soon after the collapse, the remaining portion of the panel was removed, carefully encased in plaster of Paris by a conservator and moved to the park research center. The plaster preservation research that resulted is discussed in the chapter on Mug House.

On the positive side, Step House has benefited from two recent research projects, the re-dating of tree ring samples from the Wetherill Mesa collection, and a documentation and condition assessment of rock art in 65 archaeological sites in the park. The recent reexamination of the Step House tree ring collection by the Tree-Ring Laboratory gives a date of 618-626 for the six pithouses, with four dating to the period 618-621, and two to 626. The pueblo dates to 1226-1240. These dates are based on 173 dated tree ring samples. There are numerous cutting dates from the pithouses but only two from the pueblo.

Rock Art

In August 1996 I watched a wall of flames sweep up Soda Canyon torching all vegetation in its path, and modifying all the sandstone that it touched – including the sandstone butte of Battleship Rock which is the location of one of only two mas-

Mesa Verde National Park

Lena DeTar documenting rock art at Petroglygph Point in 1999.

sive rock art panels in the park (the other is Petroglyph Point on Chapin Mesa). On that day I vowed that in the future something would be done to record and better protect rock art.

The rock art documentation and assessment program, led by Four Corners Rock Art Specialist Sally Cole, started small with assessing the damage to rock art from the fire. It expanded over the next few years and in 2000 a four-year project to locate, document and assess rock art in a minimum of 10 sites per year began. Step House, which has some very visible and interesting rock art – carved and painted images on rock as well as the images painted on plaster – was one of the 65 sites covered by this research.

Nordenskiöld published a photograph of a boulder covered with petroglyphs in Step House and had a chapter on paintings and rock markings. He mentioned plastered walls with floor bands "bordered at the top with

Left: Petroglyphs at Step House. Right: Drawing of the petroglyphs by Sally Cole.

triangular points" and spirals, zigzag lines and "the primitive manner of
delineating human figures." Nusbaum was obviously not interested in rock
art, but Nichols, in his unpublished manuscript, mentioned "several
black X's and T's and parallel streaks apparently made by daubing the
fingers in mud and drawing the tips across the cave roof" above Pit
Structure II. In his section on Kiva A he described the wall painting
which "extends across northwest quarter on lower liner wall from second
to fourth pilasters, dark reddish-black from floor level to 1.3 feet above,
white up to banquette: 4 sets of 3 dark triangles extend into white portion from dark band; row of 9 bighorn sheep etched into white band, 2.2
feet above floor, between pilasters 2 and 3." In the same discussion of
Kiva A he stated that the lower kiva liner was covered with 25-30 coats
of plaster.

The 2004 report on the documentation and assessment of the rock art
in Mesa Verde National Park has some fascinating information on Step
House (this report does not include information on the bighorn sheep
panel since it had been removed before this research). The rock art in
Step House is located on 15 rock panels, two plaster panels, and 10
masonry panels. In Step House human, animal and geometric images
include a flute player, a splayed-leg human figure, a spiral, and possible
stars. This is one of the sites the project's Hopi consultants visited. They
interpreted the crosses (stars) and streaks on the alcove ceiling as *sootu* –
"celestial object, Milky Way" – and the pecked, incised, and grooved
images of humans and geometrics on a boulder room wall as *navoti'at*,
meaning "their knowledge." The stars and streaks are above rooms of the
cliff dwellings and were drawn either while standing on roofs of these
buildings or on the alcove ledge just behind the cliff dwellings. These
stars may in fact date back to either the Basketmaker III or the Pueblo III

Drawing of the images on the ceiling of Step House.

occupation of Step House. In Mesa Verde this clustering of stars is unique to Step House and suggests to recent researchers that "the occupants studied and recorded astronomical subjects and may have been specialists in the field" with the alcove serving as a "planetarium."

Conclusion

Step House is an important site for many reasons. It is a multi-component site where the two components, Basketmaker III and Pueblo III, can be easily seen and distinguished. It has a unique excavation history, the park's only reconstructed pithouse, the only prehistoric stairway and some of the park's most fascinating rock art. It does not have the compelling appearance of Cliff Palace or Long House, so in fact it is a great place to spend some quiet – even solitary – time in a shaded alcove on a hot summer afternoon having the undivided attention of the park interpretive ranger on duty in the site.

Recent panoramic image of Kiva A, Step House.

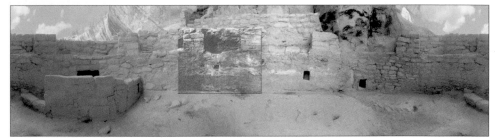

Historic image superimposed over recent image, showing one section of the plaster panel before it fell.

Digital recreation of a section of the Kiva A plaster panel based on historic photographs.

MUG HOUSE: MUGS AND MOIETIES

August 3, 1995: Three Zuni Pueblo elders are visiting a cliff dwelling for the first time. It is Mug House because students from the pueblo have been working there. They are talking excitedly between themselves in a language I do not understand, but their hands and facial expressions make it clear they can hardly believe what they are seeing – finger impressions in mortar, decorated plaster, and door loops – all original. They can almost touch their ancestors.

Introduction

Mug House is not open to the public, not even in the summer, but it is accessible. There is a very readable report covering the excavation of this site in 1960-61. Long House and Mug House are the only cliff dwellings in Mesa Verde benefiting from published reports on modern multidisciplinary, controlled excavations. The result is that we know much more about these sites than any of the others. Also, information from these sites makes it possible to infer what was taking place in other cliff dwellings at the same time. One of the preservation projects with which I was most involved was initially centered in Mug House.

Mug House was named by the Wetherills for a cluster of mugs they found tied together in these ruins in the winter of 1889-90. There is an inscription in the rear of Mug House, "Wetherill 1890." For them, no site

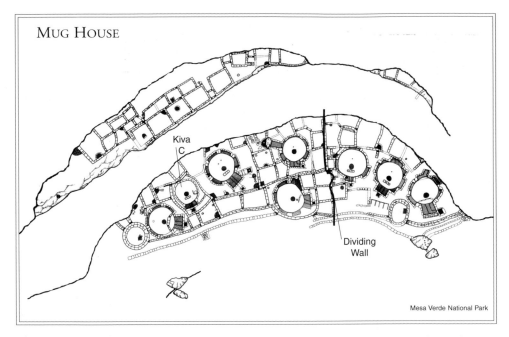

MUG HOUSE

Kiva
C

Dividing
Wall

Mesa Verde National Park

yielded so much "stuff" in proportion to its size, yet excavation in the early 1960s proved they didn't find all the objects left behind by the original occupants. Mug House is one of the typical mid-size cliff dwellings on the west side of Mesa Verde National Park. It contains approximately 100 defined spaces – ceremonial rooms, towers, storage rooms, courtyards, dwelling rooms, mealing areas, and terraces.

Like the other cliff dwellings, it evolved with no preconceived plan. The alcove is 220 feet long by 42.5 feet deep. The site is on three levels with two ledges within the alcove 16 feet above the main portion of the site. Rooms of various functions are located on both the floor of the alcove and the larger ledge. All four rooms on the small ledge are for storage. There is no spring in this west-facing alcove. The closest springs are 1.5 miles to the north or a half mile to the south, below Jug House. Down-canyon from the site 200 feet is a reservoir that was undoubtedly built and used by the occupants of Mug House. It is 23 feet long by 10 feet high by 3 feet deep and could hold about 600 gallons of water, collected as it runs off the slick-rock on the mesa top.

Gustaf Nordenskiöld first made brief mention of Mug House in his *The Cliff Dwellers of the Mesa Verde*. His excavations in the site in 1891 were not extensive. He described perforated shells and two decorated pots as well as a hearth in one room. He included illustrations of several objects from Mug House at the end of the text: pottery ladle, bowls and a pitcher; stone knives, axes, hammer, and a *tchamahia*; a bone scraper and awl; a decorated piece of cotton cloth and a number of perforated shells.

Mug House was part of the West Side Expedition led by Superintendent

Mug House in 1935 before stabilization.

Nusbaum in 1928 with the goal of salvaging objects from disturbed deposits to place in the park's new museum. There is no published account of exactly where Nusbaum worked or what he removed from the site. In the 1930s Depression era, project funds were used to repair/stabilize a number of large cliff dwellings, some that were open to the public and others, like Mug House, that were not. Twenty days were spent in Mug House in 1935, the first repairs made to the site. Then in the late 1950s Mug House was selected as one of three cliff dwellings on Wetherill Mesa to be excavated during the Wetherill Mesa Project. It was excavated and stabilized, but has never been opened to the general public. Visitation levels on Wetherill Mesa have not necessitated the opening of a third cliff dwelling.

Excavation and Stabilization

Excavation and stabilization of Mug House began in 1960 and took 11 months. Walls and features were stabilized soon after their exposure. Arthur H. Rohn was in charge of the excavation and his report is a classic for that genre: well written, thoughtful, and complete. Rohn isolated three periods of occupation of the Mug House alcove, with construction from the last occupation visible today. The first occupation dates to the mid-11th century, and probably consisted of one small house unit with a living room, storage rooms and a kiva. The second occupation dates to the late

11th century. This occupation consisted of two clusters of rooms and their associated kivas. The final appearance of the site dates from 1204 through the 1270s with the majority of construction between 1250 and 1266. The last date from the site is 1276.

Rohn identified three levels of organization within 13th century Mug House based on the layout of rooms, doorways and open spaces. These levels resulted from the sharing, cooperation, and interaction of the individuals that built and lived in Mug House. At the lowest level was a suite of rooms that contained a living room with a hearth and several storage rooms, all connected by doorways. The composition of a suite changed through time with the addition and abandonment of rooms, undoubtedly due to the changing needs of the occupants. There were a minimum of 13 suites in Mug House and may have been as many as 20 at any one time. Then there were four courtyard units, each consisting of several suites plus a kiva and courtyard. The physical layout of each courtyard, and the suites of which they were made, changed through time with two kivas and three rooms vacated prior to the occupants' final departure from the alcove village. Finally, the site was divided by a wall with three courtyard units to the north of the wall and one to the south. A wall dividing a village is a common attribute in Mesa Verde cliff dwellings. It suggests a dual division of the social group living in the village. Anthropologists use the term "moiety" for such a social unit. Mug House has a tower and mealing area associated with each of the divisions. Unfortunately, the date of the wall dividing the village is unknown. A similar wall in Cliff Palace dates to late in the occupation of the site. Above the village level of organization was the community of which Mug House was only one member. The community included individuals living in vil-

WHERE WERE THE KILNS?

Broken pieces of pottery are ubiquitous on Mesa Verde and until fairly recently there had always been a question of exactly where all this pottery was fired. A pretty hot fire is needed, so a pottery kiln should be fairly easy to locate and identify, but hadn't been. Then in the mid-90s while trenches were being dug for utility lines on Chapin Mesa, the elusive kilns were located – in fact nine kilns were located and excavated. The stone-lined kilns were built away from the villages on the slopes of minor drainages. One of these is near Spruce Tree Terrace. It was preserved (backfilled after excavation) with the hope that someday it will be put on exhibit with a protective shelter and interpretive sign. To my knowledge there is no such structure on exhibit on the Colorado Plateau and yet pottery was and continues to be very important to the Pueblo people.

46 Mug House Burials Found

SEX	6 female	14 male	26 sex unknown	
AGES	0-4 years: 24	5-15 years: 4	20-25 years: 3	27 years+: 13 (2 age unknown)

lages close enough to Mug House for them to interact on a daily basis, occupants of nearby villages such as Step House and Long House.

Mug House is stabilized today. The trash and dirt from original occupants and early explorers that had accumulated over the years has been removed and the walls repaired by replacing deteriorated stones and missing mortar. During its occupation, Mug House undoubtedly looked like any modern village, with rooms being built as others collapsed and were abandoned, dirt and trash accumulating in little-used corners. Excavation made clear that room function changed through time. A storage room in one period would be converted to a dwelling space at another time.

Artifacts uncovered during excavation of Mug House reflect the occupant's main reliance on corn, most notably 105 metates and 494 manos. Corncobs were found in the trash, in room fill, and pressed into the mortar of walls. The most common man-made objects were the thousands of fragments of pottery – plain, corrugated, and painted. Mugs, jars, ollas, bowls, and whole or fragmentary ladles make it clear that water consumption and food storage and preparation were as important in the 13th century as they are today. More than 450 whole and restorable vessels have come from this site, more than from Long House, even though it is a smaller site. The 1960-61 collection included 179 jars, 170 bowls, 34 dippers, and 27 mugs. The occupants used digging sticks for planting and stone axes for cutting wood. Hammerstones and mauls were used for pounding. Arrow points, arrow shafts, fragments of bows and deer bones, as well as cottontail bones are the remains associated with hunting. Many bones of domesticated turkeys were found. Cotton cloth, yucca sandals, turkey feather blankets and sewn animal skins suggest the type of apparel worn. Ornaments, which were fairly rare, were made of bone, stone and shell.

Thirty-five burials were uncovered during the excavation of Mug House and 11 more were uncovered during the excavation of deposits in alcoves and refuse just north of Mug House. Also, human bone representing a minimum of seven individuals was found in the excavated deposits. It is not known how many burials were removed from the site prior to controlled excavation in 1960 and 1961. The earliest burials are from the south end of the site, before this area was filled with rooms and kivas. Later burials were placed in deposits at the front of the site, where trash was also deposited. The mortality rate for babies and very young children was quite high.

Objects uncovered during excavation reveal a population that was totally dependent on local resources, revealing almost no evidence of trade. These people relied on wild resources such as pigweed, goosefoot, and cottontail. But it was produce from their cultivated fields that was the basis for their economy. Corn, beans, and squash sustained them. Domestic turkeys supplied meat, feathers, and bone for tools. The occupants of the site, based on the percentage of worked bones from excavated deposits, seem to have become less reliant on deer and more on turkeys through time. Undoubtedly, though, they ate the meat of both animals.

Plaster Preservation

Many cliff dwelling walls were once plastered, and although some of the plaster has been lost for various reasons – exposure to water, wind, and abrasion – much of it still remains. Many of the plaster panels have been exposed to the elements since they were applied in the 13th century. Others were protected by the natural accumulation of dirt and debris until they were exposed during excavation. In either case deterioration does occur through time. In some cases the time frame is so long that the panels are essentially stable and will last, if the environment stays the same, for many more years. In other cases where the environment has changed for whatever reason, loss can be quite rapid.

During the Wetherill Mesa Project, excavation exposed several decorated plaster panels at Long House, Step House, and Mug House. Since exposure, some of these panels have been deteriorating quite rapidly, at a rate that can be established thanks to the many photographs taken of them from the 1960s to the present.

The problem was not unique to Mug House or Wetherill Mesa. To tackle it, we first had to define the scope of the problem throughout the park – how many plaster panels were there and what was their condition? We had to establish technique(s) for stabilizing deteriorating plasters and then train personnel in how to use them. Then we had to figure out how to fund this program. One thing was obvious – preserving plaster is very different from preserving walls. Replacing stones and mortar demands an approach to detail, but on a different scale than preserving tiny, thin flakes of plaster. So instead of stonemasons, we needed architectural fabric conservators with much patience, good hand-and-eye coordination, and an interest in earthen materials.

Two things then happened that focused park managers' attention on plaster preservation. First, a large section of the plaster panel of nine bighorn sheep detached and fell to the floor in Kiva A in Step House. This was a great loss as it was one of the most complex narrative panels in the

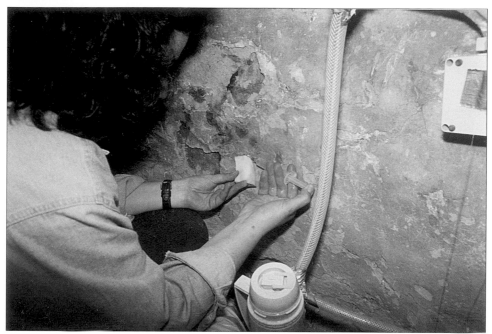

Rynta Fourie treating plaster at Mug House in Kiva C, in 1997.

park. Second, at the same time as the plaster program was evolving, a very serious problem with stone deterioration was noted in Hovenweep National Monument. The Hovenweep problem led me to Frank Matero of the University of Pennsylvania's graduate program in historic preservation. While discussing the stone problem with Matero, it became clear that he was even more interested in earthen plaster preservation. So the University of Pennsylvania's historic preservation program – staff, students, and consultants – became the driving force behind both problems. UPenn staff and students solved the problem of who would develop the techniques needed for plaster preservation (graduate student research projects) and then who would implement those techniques (preservation students attending a graduate level field school). My job became one of finding the funding for such a preservation program and making sure the needs of a summer field school were met: housing, transportation, work space, and such.

It was necessary first to figure out what was causing the deterioration. Then techniques for preserving plaster had to be developed – reattaching flakes, grouting areas of major detachment, removing salts and other deposits on the plaster, and finally training individuals who would, in their professional lives, address these problems. The initial work was done at Mug House for several reasons. In 1983 it was the location of one of the earliest experiments with plaster preservation in the Southwest. A lot was known about the history of plaster deterioration in the site through a series

John Fidler checks environmental monitoring of Kiva C, Mug House in 1997.

of very good photographs going back to the original excavation in 1960. The plaster in Kiva C was important because there were multiple decorated layers. Detachment, one of the most common and serious problems with plaster in Mesa Verde, was at its most extreme there. Also, the site was accessible and yet not open to the public, so work would not be disruptive to the park's interpretive program.

In all, six years were spent working on the plasters of Mug House. Matero brought in experts in architectural fabric conservation – conservator, architect, and engineer – from a preservation group, English Heritage, who designed a system to study the environment of Kiva C in Mug House (moisture, wind, sun) and relate their data to the obvious problems of stone, mortar, and plaster deterioration. After many square feet of loose plaster was reattached at Mug House, the program moved to Cliff Palace and then Spruce Tree House. Monitoring of this work will continue indefinitely, establishing not only how successful the present approach to reattachment is but also allowing the park to create a maintenance cycle for this resource. A dilute solution of gelatin was used as the glue holding the plaster flakes in place and the grout was a mixture of clay, water, and microspheres injected into voids in the plaster with large syringes like those used by large-animal veterinarians.

At one point during this project, students from Zuni Pueblo in New Mexico came to Mesa Verde to work with the University of Pennsylvania students. The Zuni were so excited about the work they brought their tribal elders to see the project. These men were amazed – with the site, the work, and the landscape. Other students on this project, mostly graduate students at the University of Pennsylvania, were from Turkey, Thailand, South Africa, Peru, Italy, France, and India, with a few Americans thrown into the mix.

Conclusion

The walls are stable, the plaster is reattached, and the weeds are cut. The clear layout of rooms, towers, mealing bins, and kivas into suites built around courtyards which are then clustered on either side of a dividing wall are uniquely visible in Mug House. It is too bad the site is not open to the public, but there is not enough demand for yet another cliff dwelling on Wetherill Mesa. Mug House raises some interesting questions. Why did this site contain so many mugs, as well as jars and bowls? Why here, and only here, was a reservoir built to capture drainage runoff at the base of a cliff?

Kidder and Nusbaum signatures at site 5MV1885.

BACKCOUNTRY: HIKING AND HELICOPTERS

June 1987: We are ready to enter 5MV1885 on the southern tip of Long Mesa. The helicopter has delivered ladders of various lengths – 10 feet, 12 feet, a 40-foot extension ladder – plus a 2 inch x 12 inch x 20 foot plank, and rope of various lengths. The ladders have been put in place and tied down. We are ready to enter FOR THE FIRST TIME this cliff dwelling that just hangs onto several ledges well above the talus slope. With visions of pots and points in our heads, we enter and see "J. Nusbaum A. Kidder Aug. 14, 1908" inscribed on the back of the sandstone cliff. So much for being the first!

Introduction

Five cliff dwellings are open to the public and five more are excavated and stabilized. All the rest – approximately 600 – are in the backcountry. Although none of these is as big as Cliff Palace and Long House, a few aren't much smaller – most notably Spring House and Double House. Most contain from one to 10 rooms, so these sites vary greatly in size. The few dated tree ring samples from small sites with fewer than 10 rooms suggest that they were built at the same time as the larger cliff dwellings, in the 13th century. Many of these sites unfortunately contain no wood for dating because the top of the alcove functions as the roof of the rooms. There is no answer – at least for now – to such an interesting question as: "Were the small storage rooms

found in the cliffs built at the same time as the cliff dwellings or were they built and used before the big move into the alcoves in the 13th century?"

Many of the smaller cliff rooms were obviously just for storage, some of them too small to even enter. Other cliff dwellings (meaning all rooms in cliffs and on cliff ledges) are small but contain individual rooms large enough to have been used for sleeping and food preparation. Since these rooms have not been excavated, the distribution of firepits in backcountry cliff dwellings is just one of many unknowns. Some small sites have associated kivas. In other areas clusters of small cliff dwellings are found in the vicinity of a site which just contains a kiva. Also, most of these small cliff dwellings are not far from mesa top sites with which they might be associated. We just don't know.

Mesa Verde National Park includes steep-sided canyons and broad mesas in the western half of the park and broad canyons and narrow ridges in the eastern portion of the park. The pattern of changing village locations through time differs dramatically in these two areas of the park. Very few Basketmaker sites have been identified both because of the subsurface type of dwelling and because many have probably been covered by later construction. In the Pueblo I period, some villages were located in the broad canyons to the east, but many more were on the western mesa tops. The Pueblo II period saw a dramatic preference for construction in the broad canyons in the eastern portion of the park. The trend was reversed in the Pueblo III period, when the early preference was for mesa tops and then

Mesa Verde National Park

**Willie Begay and Kee Charley John
work at site 5MV1885, in 1987.**

later the rush was for the alcoves in the cliffs.

When looking at a single mesa such as Chapin Mesa, we can see that site distribution changed from a concentration of sites before Pueblo II at about 7,000 feet, to a movement up-mesa to the Far View area at 8,000 feet in Pueblo II, and then the final movement back down-canyon and into the large alcoves in late Pueblo III. Small cliff dwellings, on the other hand, are found in all areas – at the upper end of canyons as well as down-canyon. Unfortunately we do not know if the small cliff dwellings were built before or at the same time as the major cliff dwellings. Are those higher in elevation associated with such PII complexes as the Far View Community or are they part of the late PIII occupation of the cliffs? And just as initial construction and occupation is an open question, there is also no date for movement away from these small ledges and alcoves.

The ease of movement between these small cliff dwellings can vary widely. In one shallow canyon in the park, School Section Canyon, movement between almost 20 sites is very easy. In 1986, I supervised two stabilization crews working in the canyon and could easily move between sites. Upper Soda Canyon was just the opposite. There the canyon is deep and although the density of these small cliff dwellings is high, it is a struggle getting into many of the sites and moving between them can take hours.

History of Stabilization

The 20th century history of these sites also varies greatly. Nordenskiöld entered and did minor excavation in 20 cliff dwellings, including Painted Kiva House near Cedar Tree Tower on Chapin Mesa with its beautifully decorated plaster panel in one of the kivas, and Ruins 16 on Wetherill

Kee Charley John at site 5MV1197. Note water and ash damage near the doorway. This was caused by a wildfire followed by a major thunderstorm.

Mesa with its rooms, towers, and kivas. In the 1910s, Fewkes cleaned up and stabilized such cliff dwellings as Square Tower House, Oak Tree House, Fire Temple, and New Fire House which are currently visible from overlooks on Mesa Top Loop Road and managed as mid-country sites, and also Painted Kiva House. Right after Fewkes' work, these sites were open to the public. However, parking and access were such problems at these loca tions that park policy changed. The sites are now only viewed from a distance, or not at all in the case of Painted Kiva House. In the 1930s with New Deal funds, many of the larger backcountry and mid-country cliff dwellings were stabilized for the first time, including many of those visited by Nordenskiöld. Many of these sites had not been excavated, but had exposed walls that were obviously unstable. Unamended mud mortars were developed and used to fill eroded mortar joints, set loose stones, and replace missing stones. Spring House, 20½ House, Double House, Sunset House, Painted Kiva House, and many others were part of this project. Photographs were the major form of documentation.

In the 1940s and '50s an archaeological survey of Chapin Mesa scoured the top of the mesa and the associated cliffs for clusters of pottery, mounds of rock, and standing walls. In the 1960s the general Wetherill Mesa Archaeological Project included a survey of Wetherill Mesa and in the 1970s the rest of the park was surveyed. With the completion of this survey,

JUST HANGING IN THERE

July 21, 1989, at Kodak House: A typical day turns into one I will never forget. My job for the day is to apply a silicone dripline to the alcove ceiling high above the cliff dwelling. This is the first time I will do this off a rope, descending down to the right level, caulk gun and silicone in hand, applying the silicone bead and then continuing on down to the floor of the alcove. One crew member is to assist me.

The rope setup is no problem. Lon goes down to sit in the upper ledge to pull me over by rope so that I can reach the area where I am to apply the silicone bead. To stop myself and free my hands, I have decided to use a jumar (a metal device that grips the rope holding the rappeller in place… but requiring upper body strength to release). So far so good, but then I realize that I am not strong enough to pull up my weight to release the jumar. As I am hanging off the rope with no clear idea of how to release myself, the noon hour rolls around. Since we always quit for lunch at exactly 12 noon, the crew laughs about leaving me with my problem and going to lunch.

By then my legs are numb, leading to a real moment of panic with blood rushing from my extremities. It lasts only a second. I apply the tube of silicone with shaky hands and then Lon suggests cutting the webbing holding the jumar since I have my knife. But my knife is in my back pocket and I can't get it out because the harness strap is over the pocket. He then suggests a foot loop and that works. I make a loop in the rope, put my weight on the loop and release the jumar. Then I have to release the knot creating the loop before the figure-8 descender gets to it. I just make it and then descend down to the floor of the alcove.

Wow – it is good to get back on solid ground! After that I throw away the jumar and for the last three applications, Lon pulls me over to the right position under the alcove and this is enough to stop all downward movement on the rope.

the number, size, and general condition of cliff dwellings in the park was documented. But going from there to a specific schedule for stabilization was quite a challenge. Just getting to the sites was often difficult, with poorly maintained dirt roads and long hikes. Getting stabilization materials to these sites was even more of a challenge. In the 1930s pack animals were used. In the 1980s the park turned to helicopters, which were there for wildfire suppression. With funding, in fire-free periods the helicopter pilot and crew welcomed the challenge of moving materials around the park via helicopter long-line. Barrels of water, dirt, tools, ladders, and planks were moved as close to cliff dwellings as possible. In some cases, when there was no road within reasonable walking distance, even the crew was moved by helicopter.

Next, it was necessary to decide which of the hundreds of cliff dwellings most needed work. Documentation during the park surveys was useful but

The crew works at site MV1175.
From left: Bob Yusten, Gene Trujillo, Kathy Fiero, Willie Begay and Raymond Begay.

20-year-old assessments of villages in alcoves with springs or on ledges exposed to precipitation was not. Also it made no sense economically to work on a small site with a high priority for treatment in one part of the park and then move all the gear clear across the park for a high priority site in a completely different area. So crews concentrated on clusters of sites or single large sites that were in need of treatment. Helicopter surveys of the cliff dwellings supplemented information from survey documentation.

Once sites were selected for work, provenience information was assigned (room numbers and letter designations for kivas), small transits were used to accurately draw plan and cross section maps of the architecture, room and feature information was recorded, and stabilization treatment took place, with the treatments documented photographically and in field notebooks. This was done all through the '80s, treating well over 50 sites.

As the survey data grew older and older, and the one staff member who had worked on these surveys retired, the question of where to work next became more and more difficult to answer. Then in 1989 many cliff dwellings were caught in the wildland fire which burned over much of Long Mesa and surrounding canyons. These villages became the focus of backcountry assessment and treatment for several years. This was followed, through much of the 1990s, by other projects related to damage to cliff dwellings by a seemingly endless series of major wildland fires. Finally, in the late 1990s funds were available for a detailed assessment of the condition of all the cliff dwellings, large and small. This condition assessment project continues into the new century and will never really be completed since conditions of sites can change, in some cases quite rapidly as in the case of sites in wet alcoves or those impacted by wildland fire.

During the initial assessment of sites by project crews, the site is mapped with transit and tape, any datable wood is sampled, standardized forms are completed on each room, kiva, and open area, with condition of all site fabric documented, including the stability of any trash areas. If the site will benefit from a modification to its alcove dripline, a bead of silicone is applied to the lip of the alcove. The information acquired during this assessment process is then used by the stabilization staff to prioritize their work for the coming year. All depends, of course, on funding both for assessment work and treatment. But finally there is a way to make plans based on more than just 20-year-old condition comments on site survey forms and a general photograph of a few walls in a cliff dwelling. Even more important, the park is finally accumulating the information which will allow 21st century archaeologists to answer some of the questions about the distribution, function, original construction, and abandonment of the park's numerous small cliff dwellings and their relationship to the larger cliff dwellings and mesa top villages.

6

THE OTHER MESA VERDE

THE MESA TOP SITES: PREHISTORY ON TOUR
August 14, 2000: I view Wetherill Mesa for the first time after the devastating Pony Fire. The burned area is like a moonscape – not a blade of green grass, not a live tree. Ash several inches deep swirls around and fills my nose and lungs at the least little breeze. It is truly unbelievable, even compared to the other three devastating wildfires I've lived through in the park.

Introduction

I n Mesa Verde National Park there are two places to view the changing styles of kitchen, house, and village design from 600 to 1300. In the 1950s the Chapin Mesa Loop Road was opened. Archaeological sites had been selected for excavation to represent a sequence of development with a first stop at the earliest home style to the latest at the last stop. This "tour" is designed for the automobile and a booklet guides visitors along the way. High points are the park's best preserved early pithouse at Stop 1, a spectacular view of Navajo Canyon and Square Tower House from an overlook at Stop 2, and then a series of pithouses which get deeper and deeper through time and gradually take on the characteristics of kivas. The early above-ground storage rooms change into more substantial stone-walled living rooms and some of the park's earliest towers and double-coursed masonry walls dating to 1074.

At Sun Point Pueblo a standard Mesa Verde kiva with a southern recess and six pilasters is visible and it is connected to a tower by a tunnel. The highlight of the tour is what I consider one of the great overlooks in the park service: the view across Fewkes and Cliff canyons taking in Sun Temple and 12 cliff dwellings, including Cliff Palace, in this breathtaking setting. The last stop is at Sun Temple, an apparently incomplete building with massive core-veneer walls, wall stones carefully pecked to shape, and planned construction.

The Badger House Community "tour" on Wetherill Mesa was designed in the 1980s as a walking tour. A road loops the community with a scheduled tram dropping people off and picking them up at designated locations. This tour includes an early pithouse and several above-ground villages of varying ages. Again, a guide booklet is critical to understanding the community and its evolution through time. A very large, dirt-walled subsurface feature which was probably a community building (termed a great kiva by archaeologists) is unique to this tour. It is the only early great kiva on exhibit in the park.

Another unique feature seen in Badger House Community is a village surrounded by a wood palisade. A series of postholes and deteriorated wood fragments surrounding a portion of the village were spotted by archaeologists during excavation. To facilitate interpretation, the stabilization crew placed small sections of wood posts, charred at the end, into the post holes. Then at the 13th century village of Badger House, one village is clearly superimposed on an earlier village. And associated with this later village is a tunnel which connects a tower to the village kiva, the longest tunnel in the park at 15 yards.

Above: Pithouse B in 1941.
Right: Ground Plan and sections of Pithouse B in 1941.

Ground plan and sections of Pit House B

Chapin Mesa and the Twin Trees Community

Fall, any year between 1986 and 2001: the guys and I are at Stop 1 on Chapin Mesa Loop Road, staring at our most dreaded job. We have the needed tools in hand: big pipe wrench, socket wrench, bucket full of nuts, 8-foot step ladder, shovel, gloves, and a determined expression on our faces. Our heaviest sledge hammer is on hand if needed. I watch as the guys move here and there jockeying for position. None of them wants me for a partner. I'm the weakest link.

Near a cluster of early pithouse villages, two trees have grown together creating a natural graft. Inevitably, the villages have been named for this natural phenomenon. Sites in the Twin Trees area were excavated in 1947-48. Then in 1950 the park staff conducted additional excavations: two overlapping pithouses (Deep Pithouses) that fit into the sequence between Pithouse B and Twin Trees (700); Site 16, a complex of three overlapping villages (900 to 1075); and finally, Sun Point Pueblo, a

Pueblo III masonry village with a tower and kiva connected by a tunnel. The tower wall stones are great examples of stones shaped by pecking. Unfortunately, only the foundation stones of the masonry pueblo remained. Archaeologists speculated that the wall stones had been reused in one of the nearby cliff dwellings. With the excavation of this site, the mesa top interpretive loop was complete.

The early pithouse on this loop is the best preserved in the park, protected by a sturdy and appropriately sized shelter for many years. During my tenure, the pithouse floor suffered a little damage from a leaky roof one season, but the roof was soon repaired. The most memorable event was an episode of vandalism in which someone entered the site and removed the metate that was on the structure floor. In the course of their vandalism, the thieves damaged a section of wall. Dirt-walled structures are incredibly fragile and great care must be taken in entering them. When the floors are swept and garbage removed, crew members carefully avoid the edges of features. Vandals are not so careful.

People and animals have inflicted other damage on sites in the Twin Trees Community as well. Squirrels have been and continue to be very active in Site 16. Smoke bombs, mothballs, a repellent and live trapping were all tried without much success. Both Site 16 and Deep Pithouses have had stones pushed over by vandals and the skylights in the shelter over Deep Pithouse have leaked since the day they were installed.

Shelters

J.W. Fewkes was the first archaeologist to excavate a dirt-walled mesa top site in Mesa Verde National Park. Earth Lodge A was excavated in 1919 and covered with a wooden shed, the first archaeological site shelter in the park. The site was damaged when the shelter collapsed during the winter of 1940-41 and, after further testing of the archaeological deposits around it, was backfilled in 1941.

Thus began an 80-year history of successes and failures with shelters over excavated mesa top archaeological sites in Mesa Verde. Over 20 "temporary" and "permanent" shelters have been built. These shelters have varied from informal structures built by the stabilization crew out of on-hand materials, such as two-by-fours and corrugated metal sheets, to structures designed by architects for the specific needs of the park. There are presently 12 shelters in the park. Two are informal "temporary" shelters built by park staff over sites that are not on exhibit. The other 10 shelters are over sites on exhibit and were designed by architects. One is of metal, built in 1969, and is over the pithouse at Stop 1 on the Chapin Mesa Loop Road. The other nine shelters are constructed of pre-cast concrete with a wood roof and were built in 1984-87. The professionally designed shelters have been fairly successful in protecting the sites they cover. In 2000, a wildfire damaged the four shelters over the Badger House Community sites, but

Rolling up curtains at Badger House. Willie Begay, Kee Charley John, Gene Trujillo, Raymond Begay and Lon Ayers.

SHELTERING THE SITES

Every crew needs a mechanic/inventor for solutions to frustrating problems. "Our" mechanic Bob, who unfortunately retired before I did, kept our decades-old stabilization truck, Ol' Yeller, running. But his biggest coup was related to the shelters. The architects' closure system for the pre-cast shelters was a nightmare to implement. The heavy vinyl curtains had to be raised in the spring and lowered in the fall, an almost impossible task even for 200-pound bodybuilders. They are akin to big, heavy window shades without the rollers. Instead of a simple tug to make them roll up, we had to roll them by hand, fighting their weight and bulk all the way up. Bob came up with a brilliant solution: tail pipe expanders in each end of the heavy pipe at the bottom of the curtains, attached to a socket wrench. With one person on a ladder at each end of the curtain and two toward the middle on ladders using ropes and a pulley system to carry the weight of the curtain, they could roll it up tightly. I still wasn't strong enough but the other crew members became quite adept at the job.

the pithouse and stone-walled villages they protected were not damaged. Maintenance of the sites protected by these permanent shelters continues. Rubbish that has fallen into deep features is removed, the areas are swept, and damage from rodents and visitors is repaired. The siding for the shelters is installed and removed each year, at which time they are checked for potential problems.

Prior to the construction of the "permanent" metal and pre-cast shelters, post and sheet metal structures barely covered the pithouses, kivas and rooms. In some instances, rodents built tunnels nearby, creating a channel through which rainwater flowed onto the pithouse floors.

The worst problems, though, were in Badger House Community where the "temporary" structures really were designed to be temporary, so were made of two-by-fours and sheet metal. One snowy winter several of these structures collapsed, causing severe damage to many of the dirt walls. Portions had to be rebuilt before the sites were opened to the public in 1987, which was not an easy task. Raymond came up with the idea of using adobe bricks set in a mud mortar as the supporting structure. This adobe wall was built in line with the original wall with dirt then placed behind it. Wire and mud plaster were placed over the adobe wall and finally dry dirt was pressed into the wet plaster to create the approximate appearance of the original dirt walls. A huge wall patch at the great kiva had to be redone when it started bulging. We had not allowed the "wall" to dry thoroughly before placing dirt behind it.

On the basis of the Mesa Verde experience with shelters, some things are obvious. "Temporary" shelters should not even be considered. They have a way of becoming permanent and never seem to be repaired or replaced when needed. Backfilling is a better preservation technique than temporarily sheltering a site that is to be exhibited at some unspecified time in the future. Also it is important that a shelter be designed to do what it is supposed to do: be large enough to protect the site and be as maintenance-free as possible. Skylights and fairly flat roofs have been a problem at Mesa Verde. Most importantly, it must be recognized that any shelter will need maintenance.

Bee damage at Badger House Community pithouse before repairs were done in 1997.

Wetherill Mesa and the Badger House Community

May 11, 1996, Stop 1, Badger House Community: I step through the opening between two curtains of the shelter and stand frozen in place, horrified. The walls of the pithouse are riddled with gaping holes and there are mounds of dirt on the pithouse floor. What could have happened? Close inspection makes it obvious that the larvae of ground bees had become the dinner of flickers through the winter.

This Badger House Community tour was designed to replicate the experience of the Chapin Mesa "tour through time" and it does a pretty good job of it. While there is more stabilization fabric in the walls and floors of these villages, the average visitor probably doesn't notice it. The great kiva, a palisaded village, and a long tunnel give an added dimension to the visit, and a walking tour is much more agreeable for those that have the time. The frosting on the cake is the fantastic view of the cliff dwellings of Kodak House and Long House on the tram route. The tram, of course, adds that Disneyland-ish dimension.

Ground bees: These little guys (*Anthaphora bomboidae*) lay their larvae in dirt, one of the main ingredients in Pueblo architecture, so maybe it should be no surprise that they were behind a major preservation problem. They had been digging small holes into the pilaster mortar in Step House

Badger House Community pithouse right after repairs, before new mortar is dry.

for years. Some visitors were a little distracted by them but since they were only an annoyance and do not sting, the bees and I just put up with each other. They were riddling the mortar with holes but kept their destructive activity confined to a very limited area.

Then one year they deposited their eggs in holes they excavated into the wall of the pithouse in Badger House Community. Flickers discovered the food gold mine sometime over the winter and when I returned to the site that spring the walls of the pithouse were a shambles. Large chunks of dirt had dislodged from the walls and were lying on the floor of the structure. *That* generated a response.

The park natural resource specialist helped me determine the species of bee and then what to do about them. They can only survive if there is water and they only lay their eggs for a limited number of weeks in the late spring and early summer. I was not interested in killing bees – not only does that not solve the long-term problem but it goes against park policy. So the solution for Step House was to place plastic window screening over areas where bees dig holes. Aesthetically this may not be the best answer, but it only has to be done for a few weeks and visitors are quite under-standing when informed of why it is being done. The other action was to eliminate as much standing water as possible around the sites being attacked by the bees. Controlling water in the Badger House Community area does seem to have removed the problem from the pithouse. To repair

**Petroglyphs at Battleship Rock were damaged by fire.
Notice the color change and rock spalling.**

the damage done by bees and flickers, the walls of the pithouse were built up with multiple applications of mortar. Naptha was added to the mortar to repel the insects. So far, either the naptha or the control of water is working, at least in Badger House Community.

Wildland Fires

An endless number of wildland fires have burned in Mesa Verde in the last 15 years: 1989, 1996, two in 2000, 2002, and 2003. Thousands of acres of pinyon-juniper, sage and oak have gone up in flames. Because of the concern for cultural resources, all fire lines and similar earth-moving tasks have been done by hand with an archaeologist on each crew.

After each fire, surveys of the burn areas were undertaken to evaluate the extent of fire damage. The archaeological sites in the burn areas varied from prehistoric villages to historic Navajo sweat lodges and fence lines, isolated hearths to check dams and cliff dwellings. The direct effects of the fire varied from very minimal impact on buried sites to complete loss of historic wood structures. Several rooms in cliff dwellings burned when pack rat deposits caught fire and the petroglyph panel on Battleship Rock was discolored and suffered severe damage from surface spalling. During these surveys hundreds of previously unidentified sites were recorded. The great majority of these "new" sites are farming features, check dams and terraces.

Besides damaged rock art and burned rooms, the loss of vegetation led to serious erosion problems. Moving water caused damage to unexcavated mesa top pueblos and pueblos on valley floors, while ash-laden runoff flowed over cliff dwelling walls, washing out mortar and depositing black ash on walls. There were no good results from these fires. It is nice that features previously covered with vegetation are now located and documented, but their protected and stable condition is now gone. Special projects were implemented to address this erosion of both open sites and cliff dwellings and at least reduce the rate of erosion. But these sites will never return to the condition they were in prior to the fires.

Fires are a lose-lose proposition for cultural resources, but the level of vulnerability does vary. The sites that are most vulnerable to wildfire damage are wood structures such as cabins and fence posts. Also very vulnerable to fire damage are rock art panels because of rock spalling, cliff dwellings which contain combustible material, and open sites on slopes. Less vulnerable to damage are lithic scatters and water control devices such as check dams. Those sites with the least vulnerability to fire are buried unexcavated pueblos and pithouses in relatively level settings. The type of suppression activities during a fire is as important as site type in surviving a fire. There is no question that the lack of bulldozers and other heavy equipment and the use of archaeologists on the fire lines have reduced the amount of damage to cultural resources in the park.

The 2000 Pony Fire burned across a portion of Wetherill Mesa including the area of the Badger House Community. The four archaeological sites were covered with 13-year-old precast concrete structures with vinyl curtains, which had been lowered right before the fire reached Wetherill. Fire was probably not considered during design and construction of the shelters as they were certainly not fireproof. The wood roofs were scorched but burned in only very limited areas. The vinyl curtains melted, as did the plastic skylights. Incredibly, the sites under these shelters survived fairly well. Damage was actually from rain after the fire, when walls under melted skylights were completely unprotected. The fire-damaged shelters were repaired with replacement vinyl curtains and wood/vinyl roofs.

Since there is no vegetation left to burn in that area of Wetherill Mesa, and will not be for many years, rebuilding with flammable materials seemed to be a reasonable decision. There was discussion about the six shelters on Chapin Mesa in areas that have not burned, all located in areas with high fuel loads. It was decided to reduce the fuel load around the shelters instead of replacing the vinyl curtains with a fire-proof material. In summer 2001, trees were cut around the intact shelters on Chapin Mesa. The result has been more visible shelters, on Wetherill Mesa because all the trees burned, and on Chapin Mesa because of the increased spacing between trees.

THE REST OF THE STORY: THE FAR VIEW COMMUNITY, CEDAR TREE TOWER, FARM TERRACES, AND SUN TEMPLE

Every late spring and late summer, 1986-2002 and beyond: The ground is covered with a green blanket of WEEDS – two types of thistle, globe mallow, dandelions, etc. We are prepared, each with his or her favorite hoe, and a file. It is an "easy money" day for the Navajo; a day of incredible boredom for the *belagaanas*.

Introduction

If the cliff dwellings and "tours-through-time" haven't completely exhausted the visitor, there is always the Far View Community, Cedar Tree Tower and the Farming Terraces, and Sun Temple to investigate. The Far View Community consists of several villages – Far View House, Pipe Shrine House, Coyote Village, Far View Tower and Megalithic House – and the prehistoric Far View Reservoir. Most of the Far View villages as well as Cedar Tree Tower and Sun Temple were excavated by Fewkes around 1920. His reports on this work are pretty minimal. Coyote Village was excavated in 1968-69 by the University of Colorado but the report has never been completed and published. The result is that shockingly little is known about each of these villages. Dating of all of them is frustrating. There are many dated wood specimens but the number of cutting dates can be counted on one hand. This is even the case if we add dates from excavated and backfilled sites in the vicinity of Far View House.

The Far View Community is located at the north end of Chapin Mesa at an elevation of about 8,000 feet. Somewhat farther down-mesa is the tower/kiva complex of Cedar Tree Tower which is on the mesa edge very close to a series of farm terraces that are on exhibit. Farther still down-mesa and just across the canyon from Cliff Palace is Sun Temple. I call all these "open" sites – not protected by natural or man-made shelters – and this means weeds and an unrelenting need for re-pointing of wall joints. More time is spent on Sun Temple and Far View House than all of the cliff dwellings and sheltered mesa top sites combined. Sun Temple and Far View House are large stone buildings with yards of wall joints that constantly need attention and many square feet of dirt "floors" that sprout new weeds after every rain. Weeds are controlled by hoeing, since herbicides are frowned on in the park and weed-whackers are not only less effective, but can damage wall stones. Why should we bother with weeds? They not only increase moisture near walls, but if not controlled, they will eventually obscure walls and even start growing out of them, causing cracks and weakening them.

When I arrived in Mesa Verde, the public was allowed and encouraged to climb on the walls at both Far View House and Sun Temple. Ladders were located at each site for public use. Because of this and to better seal walls, portland cement caps covered the walls of both villages. One of the first jobs I was involved with at Mesa Verde was the removal of Fewkes' concrete cap around the big kiva in Far View House and replacement with a flagstone and concrete cap.

In 1996, at the request of the park's Native American consultation group, management policy changed and walking on these walls was no longer allowed. The ladders were removed, making policy consistent throughout the park. The change had very little effect on the preservation program. These two sites continued to demand a lot of the crew's time and after the removal of the ladders much of the work was not even visible to the public. A fairly high percentage of these sites' massive walls is original, with just the wall cap and upper courses set in a concrete mortar. Consequently the mortar joints require a lot of attention, as do the wall caps, which prevent water from entering the walls. Cracks which appear must be sealed. Many of the walls of other open sites such as Coyote Village and Pipe Shrine are a single stone wide and would fall immediately if the mortar in joints washed out. Consequently, to save at least the form of these walls, most of the stones were reset in a cement mortar soon after excavation. It is much stronger and lasts longer than an earthen mortar but this material cracks and the stones come loose. It also looks hard and unattractive. But the walls still stand and they wouldn't otherwise.

WALKING ON WALLS

I really had no opinion regarding walking on the walls at Far View House and Sun Temple. Long before my time the caps of the walls had been hardened to allow for such activity. The amount of stabilization did not change with this new policy. My only concern is that no provisions have been made to allow the public to really see these sites now and it is no fun to spend hours and hours on walls that are never seen by the public. A viewing platform could easily be designed for the back side of Sun Temple. Far View House is more of a problem, since there is no vegetation high enough to screen a platform, but I'm sure with some ingenuity a platform could be designed that would have minimal impact on the landscape.

Far View House and the Chaco Phenomenon

Far View House really stands out against the background of informal clusters of rooms built with single and compound walls. There was a preconceived plan for Far View (with some later modifications). Many of the walls are double and some have rubble cores with stone veneer. The central kiva is larger than most at Mesa Verde. The ventilator shaft is slightly different (it is subfloor) and the rooms in the village are bigger than in other villages on Mesa Verde.

Fewkes excavated the 40-plus-room village with four kivas (a fifth kiva

Far View House in 1934.

in the courtyard was excavated later) from July to September 1916, before tree ring dating, so there are relatively few dated wood samples with an established provenience. The ones that do exist suggest the site was occupied from the 1100s up to about 1243 (a cutting date from an interior kiva). These characteristics suggest to researchers of Chaco Canyon and the San Juan Basin south of Mesa Verde that in its early period Far View House was a Chaco outlier. It has a lot of the appropriate elements. Besides those already mentioned, its location in a commanding position at 8,000 feet elevation, and its location within a cluster of more standard local sites, is typical of these Chaco outliers.

Other outliers in the area include Lowry Ruins in the Montezuma Valley north of Mesa Verde with 34 rooms, 3 kivas, and a great kiva; and Escalante Ruins in the Dolores River drainage, which has 25 rooms, and one kiva within the room block. Both of these sites are on Bureau of Land Management lands and open to the public. A third such site open to the public is Chimney Rock Pueblo near Pagosa Springs. It has 55 rooms and two kivas within the room blocks, and is administered by the U.S. Forest Service. These sites date from about 1050 to the early 1100s. Escalante Ruins and especially Chimney Rock Pueblo were built in topographically commanding positions. They are worth visiting just for the view. In fact there are some 200 Chaco outliers to the south, west, and north of Chaco Canyon.

Chacoan outliers are interesting sites. They have special architectural

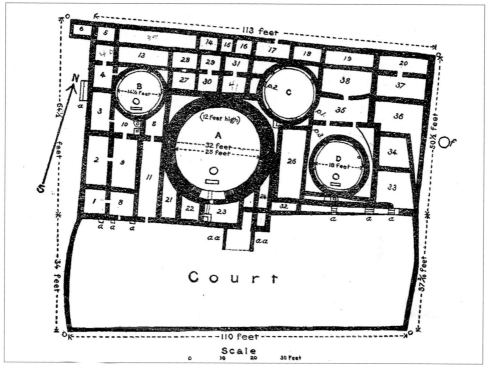

Fewkes' plan map of Far View House.

attributes and yet the artifacts found in them are locally produced, similar to nearby sites. It is fortunate for Chaco researchers that Far View House has been excavated so they can see the architecture, but unfortunate that it was cleared of rubble and artifacts before the uniqueness of such sites was established. Since Fewkes' time some work was done in the Far View area by the University of Colorado, but more is needed. It would be a great place for a major research project. Ten sites have been excavated in the area and of these, six are on exhibit. There is an adequate publication on only three of these 10 sites.

The huge Chaco Canyon sites of Pueblo Bonito, Chetro Ketl, and Pueblo del Arroyo among others were built and dominated the Pueblo world from about 850 to 1080. Salmon Ruins in Bloomfield, New Mexico, and then Aztec Ruins, in Aztec, New Mexico, came to the forefront after Chaco lost its preeminence. All of these sites are built of stone, have well over 200 rooms, are multistoried, and incorporate at least one great kiva. Salmon dates to around 1089 with no Chaco period dates after 1120, and Aztec from 1105-1115.

Chaco outliers are villages that were influenced by these central communities. Whether this influence was direct, with people from Chaco going to the outlying areas, or indirect through prestige and trends in style of con-

Weeds at Far View House Kiva A.

struction is unknown, and in fact may have differed across the landscape and through time. Wide, straight, cleared areas or "roads" are associated with the central villages and some outliers. So far no Chacoan-like road has been found on Mesa Verde.

There was a reoccupation both in Chaco Canyon and at Salmon and Aztec in the 13th century, at which time they were modified, making them more Mesa Verde-like with small kivas built within the room blocks, and big rooms subdivided to create smaller rooms. The pottery is similar to that found in 13th century Mesa Verde sites. But where did these people come from? There is no evidence of a big exodus from the Northern San Juan area until around 1280. There is evidence of a change in settlement patterns about 1240. On the Mesa Verde this is apparent with the movement into the alcoves, but even to the north and west of Mesa Verde, there was movement into canyon-oriented large villages. Larger 13th century villages are almost all located near a dependable source of water. Much work remains to be done in this area and a better understanding of the Far View Community is critical both to an understanding of the local changes in settlement patterns from 1100 to 1300 and also to the broader trends seen across the Colorado Plateau.

**Visiting stonemasons from Chaco Culture National Historical Park
are re-pointing the tower at Cedar Tree Tower.**

Cedar Tree Tower and the Farming Terraces

This little site on the edge of a Chapin Mesa drainage consists of a rectangular room and a circular tower attached to a kiva by a very short tunnel. The kiva is enclosed by a stone-outlined courtyard. A series of farming
terraces are located on the other side of the drainage that Cedar Tree Tower
overlooks. Cedar Tree Tower is one of several such small sites in the park
consisting of a very prominent tower and a stone-outlined courtyard containing a kiva. It is not a village, but rather almost certainly some special
purpose site.

Navajo Watchtower, which can be seen from Navajo Canyon overlook
on the Chapin Mesa Loop Road, is another example of such a site. There
are about 10 such sites in the park, all located on the edge of mesas. The
towers, which are the only visible feature at the unexcavated sites, are all of
double wall construction with stones pecked to shape. These are sturdy
buildings so it is not a surprise that a few are still standing. The associated
decorated pottery is Mesa Verde Black-on-white so construction for all of
these was probably late Pueblo III, 1200-1300. This is also, of course, the
period when the cliff dwellings were being built. It is interesting that
although many cliff dwellings have towers and all of the larger ones have
kivas, there are no tunnels connecting towers to kivas in the cliff dwellings.

In the cliff dwellings tunnels connect kivas to kivas, and rooms to kivas, but not towers to kivas.

On the mesa top, there are many villages which contain a tower connected to a kiva by a tunnel. Examples on exhibit include Badger House in Badger House Community, Sun Point Pueblo in the Twin Trees Community, and Coyote Village in the Far View Community. Those that are dated are Pueblo III in age. The kiva connected to the tower in Badger House has two cutting dates of 1257 and many non-cutting dates for that same year. In fact these are the latest cutting dates from a mesa top site in Mesa Verde National Park.

Mesa top sites with towers that are not connected to a kiva by a tunnel include Site 16 in the Twin Trees Community, and Pipe Shrine House and Far View Tower in the Far View Community. The third village at Site 16 is quite odd, with an oversize kiva and three towers associated with a massive-walled structure of unknown function. The one cutting date from the kiva is 1074. There are no bark dates from Pipe Shrine House but non-cutting dates vary from 865 to 1214 from the kiva and 733 to 1051 from other areas of the site.

The consensus among archaeologists is that towers became popular in the Northern San Juan area around 1100 (late PII), about the same time as pecked-face architecture. Their popularity continued through Pueblo III and ended when these people left the area. The function of the tower is not known. Those connected by tunnel to a kiva may well have been used in special kiva rituals. Their location in such special-purpose sites as Cedar Tree Tower suggest that they may also have been lookouts or possibly even observatories – a place to view the heavens – while kiva rituals were going on. What is obvious at these special-purpose kiva/tower/tunnel sites is that whatever activities took place, they were private or secret, not for the general public because they occurred inside.

Farming terraces (also called check dams), on the other hand, are ubiquitous on Mesa Verde. Almost every drainage has at least a few and some drainages have hundreds. The park also contains terraces that follow the contour of talus slopes. They are constructed of unshaped sandstone blocks from one to many courses high, built to control water and soil. Undoubtedly crops such as corn, beans, and squash were planted behind these stone terraces.

Sun Temple

This is a D-shaped, preplanned complex of 23 rooms, with an internal tower and two plaza features that look something like kivas. The walls are massive, with dirt cores covered by a veneer of sandstone blocks pecked to shape on both the interior and exterior surfaces. Sun Temple contains some of the most impressive architecture in the park, classic Pueblo III construction with beautifully shaped sandstone blocks averaging 12 to 16 inches

Sun Temple in 1935

long, 6 to 8 inches high and 6 to 8 inches wide.

We know almost nothing about this structure. Fewkes excavated the site in 1915, the first mesa top site excavated. He believed the absence of a roof and scarcity of artifacts in the fill or on the floors indicated it was never completed. Construction techniques certainly suggest a date of late Pueblo III, 1200-1300. There is a smaller version of Sun Temple, also undated, in the Horseshoe Group of Hovenweep National Monument. Another similar structure is located in Sand Canyon Pueblo in the Montezuma Valley, a town of more than 400 rooms, 90 kivas, 14 towers, a great kiva and enclosed plaza dated between the 1240s and mid-1270s.

Fewkes gave the name Sun Temple to the structure, but in fact there is no evidence that sun-related activities took place here. There is a naturally eroded basin in a sandstone boulder near the southwest corner of the structure. Fewkes made it clear that this was the original location of the boulder and it was intentionally incorporated into the structure by the builders. Because of its location, there is no way it can be used as a sundial. Fewkes said that when sitting in the shrine on September 21 he saw the sun sink below the horizon directly in front of him. Archaeo-astronomers have noted that some man-made basins just south of Cliff Palace align with the kivas in the courtyard of Sun Temple. A lot more work needs to be done on similar structures before the final word on Sun Temple is published.

7

TSE AND SLISH
PROJECTS OUTSIDE THE PARK

B etween 1988 and 2001, the stabilization crew worked outside Mesa Verde National Park on numerous "outhouse" projects. These took us as far away as Kanab and Escalante in Utah, Camp Verde in Arizona, and as close as across the Mesa Verde National Park boundary onto the Ute Mountain Tribal Park. In all cases our objective was to preserve prehistoric, and on one project historic, standing architecture. Hovenweep National Monument was a natural since the area was administered by Mesa Verde National Park.

Three projects deserve some discussion because they were the best examples of challenges in the areas of stone preservation, mortar selection, and scaffolding.

HOVENWEEP: A SCHOOL FOR STONEMASONS

October 15, 1992, Square Tower Group, Hovenweep National Monument: I am with Mary Griffitts. We are dressing up in rain coats and face masks to protect ourselves from the chemical we're using. I look over at Mary and break out laughing. She is so small that the only way she can keep the mask on is by wearing it upside down. Oh, the fun of adapting to a world designed by and for big people.

Introduction

Hovenweep National Monument is an incredible place: Clusters of free-standing towers and great houses are located in one of the most dramatic and isolated locations in the Southwest. It is much easier to envision life in 13th century Mesa Verde than in 13th century Hovenweep. When the cliff dwellings were being built on the mesa, a culturally similar group of farmers were building dams and farm terraces here, but also dramatic two-story structures on detached boulders, mesa edges, and canyon walls – all in the vicinity of reliable springs in a canyon setting.

Even more than Mesa Verde, Hovenweep is known for its towers. The most dramatic are built on large, detached boulders resting in the bottom of the drainages. Many of these buildings were so well constructed that after 700 years of exposure to snow, rain, wind, and sun, the walls are still in pristine condition, their wood roofs mostly gone but the walls standing as a tribute to their builders. The stones used to build the towers are beautifully finished by pecking. The walls themselves were often built right on the edge of boulders. In one complex two towers are built on separate boulders within a few feet of each other. Each of these towers is two stories, high above the talus. One crew member decided that in the 13th century, Hovenweep was a school for stonemasons.

This area was occupied by hunting and gathering people both before 600 and then after the 13th century, but for the centuries in between, farmers struggled to support themselves in this very dry environment. These 13th century farmers built some of the most remarkable structures

Mesa Verde National Park

Square Tower in Hovenweep National Monument. Gene Trujillo and Kee Charley John re-pointing tower, note scaffolding.

in the Southwest and had a calendrical system similar to one in Chaco Canyon. The Chaco system was in use several centuries before the one in Hovenweep.

Some major structural repairs were made to many of the Hovenweep buildings in the 1940s to stabilize them. Initially wood bracing was used, but through the years unstable sections of walls were rebuilt. In the 1960s and '70s walls were capped with a portland cement mortar, eroded footing stones were replaced and the new stones set in the same mortar. When the Mesa Verde stabilization crew returned to Hovenweep in the late 1980s, we followed a schedule of monitoring every site every two years, and filling all joints that would need it within the next 10 years – a realistic mainte-nance cycle for a park containing six groups of structures with standing architecture: Square Tower, Holly, Hackberry, Horseshoe, Cajon, Cutthroat Castle, and each of these with numerous individual buildings.

Many of the structures still have very high walls, two stories plus parapet. The structures are built right against the edge of a drainage so scaffolding of one exterior wall has to be placed on the very uneven canyon floor or on the top of a talus with detached rubble thrown in to add to the challenge. When I started on the stabilization crew, the park already had a stack of typical blue scaffolding which is great for high walls built on a level surface, including many at Hovenweep. We could tie a crew member down so he wouldn't accidentally fall, give him a hard hat and a rope for raising and lowering materials to someone below and he was ready for work.

The challenge was those walls built on the edge of the bedrock. On the canyon side of the Twin Towers structures, we improvised with ladder jacks. The most challenging aspect of this system was to get the rungs of the two ladders at relatively the same level so the plank was level. Since the terrain on which the ladders were set was so uneven, at times one ladder was set many feet higher than the other. The other challenge was to get the ladders and planks in place. Crew members had to initially set up safety ropes without being attached to any. Once the initial safety ropes were in place, then the tense moments were past. Ropes with buckets attached to one end were used to raise and lower mortar, water and chinking stones.

Stone Preservation

Square Tower is a spectacular free-standing tower, not to be confused with the cliff dwelling village of Square Tower House in Mesa Verde. It was built over 700 years ago on a detached boulder in the bottom of Little Ruin Canyon. Floors and roof are gone but otherwise the structure is in fantastic condition. On one memorable evening in September 1990 I was stunned when I looked up at the contact of the boulder and the base of the tower. The soft Dakota sandstone on which it was built had a huge cavity in it, extending back into the heart of the boulder and leaving the northeast corner of the tower completely unsupported. Light could be seen under the footing stones.

Mesa Verde National Park

**East face of Square Tower at Hovenweep National Monument in 1995.
Note the deterioration of the boulder near the center of the photo.**

The site is situated adjacent to the main drainage at the foot of the canyon, not far downstream from the perennial spring. In 1960, with water eroding the rock and threatening to topple the tower, the park service constructed a protective wall of local sandstone set in portland cement mortar. Then, with the tower obscured by overgrowth and forgotten as personnel changed over the next 30 years, nature went to work. When the vegetation was cut in 1990, it was apparent that the park service wall, far from staving off the erosion, had possibly accelerated it. Calcium sulfate deposits on the boulder and wall meant either the natural bonding material in the sandstone was dissolving or salt from the concrete was eating its way in – or both.

Action was needed to save the tower. Runoff patterns were modified to direct water away from the boulder and the deep cavity between the wall and the boulder was filled with natural mud mortar to keep out water. Meanwhile, an advisory group drawn from the park service, other agencies and private contractors created a list of short- and long-term actions, including photographic documentation of the tower in case it should fall.

There were inevitable complications. Excavation for a French drain uncovered a well-preserved kiva just below the surface, so the plan was

172   T S E   A N D   S L I S H   P R O J E C T S   O U T S I D E   T H E   P A R K

White Hair and All

In 1997 one of the worst moments of my professional career occurred. I was finishing up with the last application of ethyl silicate when it started to rain. I hadn't seen the storm coming as I was down in the canyon, but I really wasn't that concerned. I completed what I was doing, cleaned up and left.

The next day as the crew and I were leaving Hovenweep with our work for the season completed, I decided to look a last time at Square Tower to make sure I had collected everything and just to view this very spectacular tower. I looked down and the boulder was white. I found out later that when water strikes wet ethyl silicate, the chemical crystallizes. I'm sure I had heard this at some point in the past but it certainly hadn't sunk in.

I was panicked – after all of this work the boulder was probably in worse condition now than when we had started. I knew that we did not want to make the boulder's outer surface impermeable. Since the boulder is seated in a drainage bed with a spring at its head, it absorbs moisture and this moisture has to be allowed to dissipate. If not, it will build up at this barrier and erosion will take place at the interface between the boulder and the impermeable surface. I was afraid I had just done exactly that.

In fact, after many panicked phone calls to conservators and the chemical company and a field visit and testing by a conservator, it was decided that the deposit was very thin and not continuous and would weather away naturally. That is, in fact, what happened. I was left with more gray hair and a lesson learned – one needs to know what one is doing in the conservation field as in most professional fields. I was way out of my realm of expertise and it was only luck that the resource didn't suffer because of it.

scrapped. Instead, the kiva was reburied to protect it from the elements. Ceramic pins were installed in three places on the boulder to monitor surface erosion. And, on the recommendation of the conservator, deep voids in the sandstone were packed with hydrated hydraulic lime and sand, a dry, natural mixture softer than the rock itself (harder materials like concrete tend to accelerate erosion). Several stones were removed from the 1960 protective wall and no erosion was noted behind them – a good sign meaning the erosion was a surface phenomenon. The stones were reset in a natural mud mortar for easy removal and checking in the future. The joints in the tower's stonework were filled with a mud mortar amended with acrylic polymer. Al Decker, who built the stabilization wall in 1960, could remember little of the specific rationale behind its construction. The obvious concern in the 1960s was that the boulder was being undermined by flash flood erosion in the drainage, which could lead to the tower's collapse. But the result of setting the stone wall in portland cement mortar and putting more cement behind the wall had been a wall that was more impermeable to moisture than the surrounding sandstone, so moisture moved through the sandstone boulder and eroded away the binding material in the sandstone.

With erosion, sandstone grains flake off to the touch, so Mesa Verde geologist Mary Griffitts tested options and, after three years of study, chose ethyl silicate as a consolidant to keep the binder in the sandstone from eroding away. Meanwhile, a detailed photographic and graphic documentation of the sandstone surface was made and salts were removed from the problem area by poulticing. Application of ethyl silicate to the boulder started in 1996 and continued in 1997. Now the boulder is being monitored, checked yearly by various methods to determine the rate of deterioration.

The ethyl silicate has definitely hardened the boulder, but the real cause of the deterioration has not been addressed. Rain falls and the stream still flows into Little Ruin Canyon, with the water table only inches below the surface of the drainage much of the year. The rate of erosion has been reduced, but only monitoring will tell how much and how long-lasting this effect will be. All of the short-term recommendations have been carried out, but long-term preservation of the boulder and the precious piece of our nation's heritage perched precariously upon it will only be determined by time.

SLISH AT CHIMNEY ROCK

1995, about 6:30 p.m., Ute Campground at the base of Chimney Rock: I've washed and am reading a book in front of my camper before preparing dinner. I look up and into the eyes of a mature brown bear. He seems as surprised to see me as I am to see him. We look at each other and before I can even think to call the other crew members so they too can see this beautiful animal, he continues on his way walking back into the woods.

Introduction

Chimney Rock is one of those absolutely incredible places that expand the definition of landscape. A pueblo commands the high ground on a south-sloping mesa well above the Piedra River. To the north are the much higher San Juan Mountains and to the south the much lower San Juan River basin.

Chimney Rock Pueblo is a Chaco outlier – no question about that. It commands the heights, with the massive-walled pithouse-like dwellings of the locals spread out helter-skelter below. The pueblo has approximately 50 rooms and two Chaco-like kivas within the room block. Tree ring dates place construction between 1076 and 1093 although it well may have been occupied into the 12th century. Archaeo-astronomers point out that at the lunar standstills in 1076 and 1093 the moon would have risen between the two natural pillars near the pueblo.

This pueblo and the associated indigenous structures were the last structures built by farmers in this drainage. The pottery associated with all of these structures is the typical Pueblo II pottery found north of the San Juan River – in Mesa Verde as well as here on the Piedra – Mancos Black-on-white.

Mortar additives

April 1994: I'm in Rome, Italy, attending a five-month preservation course made possible by a couple of grants and the goodwill of my supervisor. I walk by the Coliseum and along the edge of the Circus Maximus on my way to class. My roommate is from South Africa and my classmates are from all over the world. On this day I'm given a note telling me to "call the office." I return the call and am told the mortar used at Chimney Rock the preceding fall was a complete bust. It is, after just one winter, soft to the touch, flaky. The whole project will have to be redone!

> "I STARTED MAKING PATTIES WITH ALL TYPES OF SOILS AND
> CONCENTRATIONS OF THE ACRYLIC POLYMER.
> … I EVEN PLACED PATTIES IN WATER AND A FREEZER
> FOR VARIOUS PERIODS."

I did not understand acrylic polymers for many years. Sometimes the mortar became hard and would last. Other times it lost its cohesion almost immediately. There were always so many variables that could affect the final result: cold episodes, snow loads, and application techniques. The possibilities seemed to be limitless. This all came to a head in 1994 when the work we had done for the U.S. Forest Service at Chimney Rock in the fall of 1993 was a complete failure. Our six-month-old mortar was flaky, completely unconsolidated. We had used the same mortar additive that we had been using in Mesa Verde for years, and yet here it was a disaster.

Conservators, chemists, soil scientists, and preservation archaeologists offered different probable causes. The acrylic polymer was used and applied when it was too cold (it had been a cold fall). It was no longer any good (but then it worked at Hovenweep just before the Chimney Rock project). The soil was too clayey and the bonds around the particles were not formed. We used too high a concentration of the polymer or we used too low a concentration. The soil was too acidic or the soils were expansive. The chemical company felt that the bonds didn't form because it was either too dry or too cold. I was frantic.

I started making patties with all types of soils and concentrations of the acrylic polymer, something I had done before to match wall color. I had never tested the effectiveness of various concentrations of acrylic polymer or its use with various soil types. Now I even placed patties in water and a freezer for various periods. At about the same time a graduate student in conservation studied acrylic polymers as additive to dirt mortars. We both came to the conclusion: A very sandy soil was needed to produce the strongest mortar. The higher the sand content is (up to all sand), the more durable the patty will be. The higher the clay content, the less durable the patty when left out in the weather. So the solution for Chimney Rock was either a soil mix with a much higher sand content if we wanted to use an acrylic polymer, or an entirely different mortar additive. Their location on the high, exposed mesa of Chimney Rock – subjected to much snow and rain, high winds and blazing sun – made unamended dirt mortar out of the question for the walls we were re-pointing.

Now that we knew the parameters, the Forest Service archaeologist actually selected the additive. The acrylic polymer was continued on the massive walled sites below the Pueblo because mortar color was critical in maintaining their appearance. The walls of these sites have wide joints between the unshaped stones and an acrylic polymer does not change the color of the soil. On the main project for 1994, the re-pointing of Chimney Rock Pueblo, calcium aluminate, a cement, was selected as the additive for the dirt mortar mix. This had been used very successfully on the Pueblo many years before. The problem with calcium aluminate is that it gives the mortar a gray color. Fortunately, mortar color on the Pueblo was really insignificant because the mortar joints are so narrow the color of the wall is set by the stones, not the mortar.

This research also helped us with our mortar at Mesa Verde, where the mesa top soils used to build the walls are red loess with high clay/silt content. For these sites the color needs to be red but the local red soil is not good with an acrylic polymer additive. In the cliff dwellings, on the other hand, the light tan soils used in their mortar have a high sand content and so work well with an acrylic polymer. So for mesa top sites, we kicked up the percentage of sandy soil and learned to live with a mortar which was not quite as deep red as we would have preferred.

The need for a high sand content in mortar is not the only problem with an acrylic polymer. As was even obvious before the Chimney Rock disaster, an acrylic polymer must dry, which it won't do in a constantly wet environment. Although not a serious problem at Chimney Rock, it is a fairly common situation at the base of walls in Mesa Verde. Since this is also a place where unamended mortars are a complete failure, there really is no present solution to the problem. Plaster conservators have been experimenting with lime mortar in a wet wall in Cliff Palace.

Talking to chemical companies about soil mortar additives is really interesting. These chemicals/cements are produced by companies for modern construction needs. Calcium aluminate was developed to be used in a very hot environment, and the acrylic polymer used as an additive at Mesa Verde was developed to be added to concrete to increase its flexibility and reduce cracking. So when I would talk to representatives of these companies, they had no expertise in the area of my interest. They were interested in the problem, but not familiar with the material. The increasing use of architectural fabric conservators trained on and interested in southwestern prehistoric architectural fabric has been a big help. These people have the knowledge of chemistry and material science AND a familiarity with the resources.

LADDER JACKS AND ROPES AT MONTEZUMA CASTLE

October 1997: An architect from the State Historic Preservation Office (in Arizona) has complained that mortar used in the Castle in 1996 looks too new. I discuss with him what we have been doing and offer to take him up to the work site. He takes one look at all the ladders needed to get up to the site and then the scaffolding perched in front of the cliff dwellings, and sits back down, shaking his head. Needless to say, he loses all credibility with the crew and with me.

Introduction

Montezuma Castle is perched high above the Verde River in central Arizona. Constructed in a limestone cliff alcove, the village is three stories high and in pristine condition. It is located just off the major freeway between Phoenix and the Grand Canyon – the restroom stop for tour buses. Because of this, it has one of the highest visitation rates in the Southwest, and the highest in relation to the number of employees. Visitors get a treat, both the lush growth of trees, grasses, and shrubs, and then the impressive village itself. In the days of low visitation, park visitors were allowed to go up into the site, ascending ladders and following trails with railings. Today there are just too many visitors and a concern about their impact on the site – particularly the need for trails, railings and much more aggressive stabilization to make sure it is safe for them.

The farmers of the Verde Valley made different tools and pots, and had a somewhat different history than those to the northeast on the Colorado Plateau. So instead of being classified by archaeologists as Anasazi (Pueblo), these people are called the Sinagua. The name – Spanish for "without water" – is not particularly appropriate for the people living in the Verde Valley where the perennial Verde River supplied plenty of water. The people were in fact named for their relatives to the north in the Flagstaff area where water was a problem. Although the roofs of the 20 or so rooms in Montezuma Castle are mostly intact, the wood is not datable. The trees used to build them were raised in a wet environment, which caused the formation of fairly uniform growth rings. With no pattern of narrow and

Montezuma Castle during stabilization.

wide rings, there is no unique sequence of rings and so, no dating. On the basis of architecture and pottery and other artifacts a frustratingly general date of 1150 to 1400 has been assigned to the village. Migration out of this area occurred around 1400, a hundred years after the Northern San Juan area out-migration.

Scaffolding

We thought Hovenweep offered the most challenging scaffolding problems until we saw Montezuma Castle in 1996. The three-story cliff dwelling is built in an irregular alcove high up in a limestone cliff. The limestone is soft and friable, and there is only a very narrow shelf on the cliff face below the cliff dwelling.

"... THESE PEOPLE ARE CALLED THE SINAGUA. THE NAME – SPANISH FOR 'WITHOUT WATER' – IS NOT PARTICULARLY APPROPRIATE FOR THE PEOPLE LIVING IN THE VERDE VALLEY ... THE PEOPLE WERE IN FACT NAMED FOR THEIR RELATIVES TO THE NORTH IN THE FLAGSTAFF AREA WHERE WATER WAS A PROBLEM. "

The front wall of the village needed to be re-pointed but there was no way ladders or scaffolding could be placed on the talus because it was too far below the site. So the only answer was to set two 40-foot extension ladders on the narrow shelf, then place ladder jacks on the ladders. The crew had been working off planks set on ladder jacks since their first use at Hovenweep in 1992 so that was not a new approach to scaffolding. To secure the ladders on the limestone shelf, we set ring bolts with long shafts into the cliff face just above the shelf, then tied the ladder base to them. Near the top of the ladders, rope was used to tie them in place. The jacks were firmly attached to the ladders, then two boards were tied to the jacks.

Two crew members, each in a harness tied firmly into place and wearing a secure hard hat, worked off the planks. A pulley was rigged up to get mortar from the talus to the upper level of the cliff dwelling. This mortar was then lowered to the workmen. It worked beautifully and due to the care taken in padding the dwelling/ladder contact, did no damage to the cliff dwelling. The ring bolts were left in place to be used the next time the face of the structure needs to be repaired.

8

Conclusion

September 29, 1995: I am at the funeral of a former Navajo stabilization crew member. His daughter is giving the eulogy about her father. She says that he died and was revived before his final death. She asked him what heaven was like. He said that it was like Mesa Verde with lots of trees.

M esa Verde has had over 20 million visitors in the past 100 years – 27 tourists came in 1906 and over half a million in the last few years. Most visitors love their few hours in the park. The beautiful environment and the captivating cliff dwellings leave people quite impressed. It is relatively easy to imagine living in a cliff dwelling with its courtyards, rooms, and doorways. There are those who ask such questions as: "Where did they go to the bathroom?" and "Why didn't they build closer to the highway?" But the important questions about water and food are rarely asked. We have become so detached from our environment that we just assume these critical resources are always available. That is why a trip to Mesa Verde continues to be so important – to teach us about our past and place us back into our environment. Preservation and education have not lost their importance in our technologically sophisticated but environmentally and historically "challenged" culture.

"THE FACTS WILL NOT CHANGE THROUGH TIME BUT INFERENCES BASED ON THEM MAY CHANGE WITH THE ADDITION OF NEW FACTS. "

What has been learned about the cliff dwellings and other villages in the last 100 years? It is important to make a distinction between **facts** that have been learned through research and **inferences** that are based on these facts. The facts will not change through time but inferences based on them may change with the addition of new facts. So what **facts** have we acquired from research over the past 100 years? The most useful gain in knowledge came from the development of tree ring dating. Based on cutting dates of wood associated with buildings and building features, the villages of Mesa Verde were built between 600 and 1280. Many of the large cliff dwellings were divided by a wall restricting access between the two parts of the villages.

Because of excavation, we know the height of individuals. These people made pottery as early as 600 and throughout their occupation of Mesa Verde. The early pottery was fairly crude and gave way to beautifully well-crafted pots in the last years of production. These are facts that will not change with more research. From these facts we **infer** that Mesa Verde was occupied between about 600 and 1280 and that final migration from the mesa occurred sometime shortly after 1280. Even one tree ring date of, say, 1290 would change this interpretation. We can calculate the average height of the adult population. We can study the jar-to-bowl ratio or calculate the number of cooking vessels versus serving vessels and determine if this ratio changed through time. The results of such studies can change with more research and the addition of new facts. But we do know things about these people. We know more than Nordenskiöld and Fewkes did, and a hundred years from now, if research continues, we will know still more.

Mesa Verde National Park has evolved from a park with only a few Chapin Mesa cliff dwellings open to the public to one with the full sequence of architectural styles, from pithouses to mesa top villages to cliff dwellings on exhibit. Sites on Wetherill Mesa have been opened as alternatives for the public. A few cliff dwellings have actually been closed after initially being open for visitation: Square Tower House, Oak Tree House, Fire Temple, and Painted Kiva House. But others have been opened: Long House and Step House. The effort to reduce congestion on Chapin Mesa by opening sites on Wetherill Mesa has not been very successful – people still want to see the most famous cliff dwellings, even though equally interesting ones await them elsewhere in the park. So Wetherill Mesa's sites remain an uncrowded getaway on a summer day.

What can we look forward to in the 21st century? I hope there will be a renewed realization of the educational importance of the park and less emphasis on recreation. Many of the park's past spectacles have had little to do with the original purpose of the villages. The trend lately has been for more consultation with culturally affiliated groups about all sorts of park projects and hopefully this trend will continue. Everyone will benefit from the added input and interest of modern Indian groups. And of course we are all excited about the possibility of a virtual tour of the cliff dwellings. In fact this shouldn't be far off and will certainly be a plus for those who, for whatever reason, aren't able to visit Spruce Tree House, Cliff Palace, and the others. But the hope that virtual tours will reduce the congestion on Chapin Mesa is probably not realistic. In fact, computer simulations could very well increase visitation. More people will know more about the cliff dwellings and want to experience them firsthand.

What about the preservation of Mesa Verde's resources? We know a few facts about preservation based on 100 years of intervention. We know that portland cement has had a negative effect on the preservation of mortar and stone. We know that an acrylic polymer does not work well with a mortar mix high in silt and clay. We know that a bead of silicone makes a great new dripline for an alcove and can last for at least 15 years. We know that ethyl silicate can be used to harden sandstone. We know that a mix containing gelatin can be used to reattach plaster flakes in the dry southwestern environment.

What about preservation in the future? Maintenance is always necessary

MY OWN VISION

In recalling the vision of Fewkes with his emphasis on education and preservation, here is my vision for the park on its 100th anniversary.

Education goals: 1) platforms have been built so the public can view Sun Temple and Far View House; 2) a pottery kiln is on exhibit in the Chapin Mesa administration district.

Preservation goals: 1) there is a permanent full-time crew to maintain the ruins and of a size and composition (archaeologists, stonemasons, conservators) so that the front- and mid-country sites remain stable and with some time left for backcountry sites; 2) the parking lot over Cliff Palace has been re-graded so the asphalt surface drains to the south and NOT into the ditch that follows the fault over the site; 3) gloves are worn by all who enter the cliff dwellings; 4) there is support for research into the history of the cliff dwellings and other villages in the park; and 5) research into preservation technology is ongoing.

and I don't expect a miracle chemical or technology to change that. But new ideas, chemicals that might reduce the amount of maintenance needed or extend the cycle seem likely. We don't know how to preserve mortar or plaster in a wet environment. Just as I was leaving in 2002, conservators started experimenting with a lime mortar. Possibly this will hold up under moisture. We don't know how to effectively control moisture in most cliff dwellings. There are all kinds of challenges for preservation specialists in the years to come.

For me it is humbling to think that I lived and worked in Mesa Verde National Park for one fifth of its existence – 20 years. I know future archaeologists and preservation staff will question or criticize what I did or did not do. Portland cement was the miracle compound that wasn't. What about acrylic polymers, ethyl silicates, and gelatin as an adhesive? How will they stand the test of time? But I can sleep at night. I had to do what I could to prevent walls from collapsing, plasters from detaching. And like Indiana Jones, that fictional archaeologist in "Raiders of the Lost Ark" whose greatest discovery was hidden away for all time, I realize many of my successes and failures will be forgotten. What will endure, I hope, are the buildings and creations of a group of people that survived and thrived for centuries in a challenging environment.

GLOSSARY

GLOSSARY

A

Abandoned, left, migrated: archaeologists have for years used the term "abandoned" when referring to what happened on the Colorado Plateau around 1280. Modern Pueblo Indians question the appropriateness of the term. They feel that their ancestors moved away but left the villages as a record of their history, a record of their clan migrations. Although their ancestors moved away, they did not abandon the villages since these villages are still important to them.

Alcove: a natural recessed area in the sandstone cliffs of Mesa Verde. The important point is that they are **natural** and were formed by both mechanical (the freeze-thaw cycling of water through the permeable sandstone and impermeable shale lenses in the Mesa Verde geologic formation) and chemical (the dissolution of the calcium carbonate in the sandstone in a wet environment) processes. The cliff dwelling of Montezuma Castle on the Verde River is also in a natural alcove but in this case in a limestone cliff.

Anasazi: from the early 20th century up until fairly recently, the Navajo word *anasazi* was used to refer to the pre-Hispanic farming cultures that occupied the northern Southwest from about the time of Christ to 1300. But descendents of these farmers prefer the term Ancestral Pueblo or Ancestral Puebloan, which is used in this book, except when quoting Navajos, who continue to use the term *anasazi*. When referring to historic documents, the term used in them – almost always Anasazi – is used.

Anthropology: the study of mankind with four main subdivisions: cultural anthropology, archaeology, physical anthropology, and linguistics. Cultural anthropologists and archaeologists focus on understanding the full spectrum of world cultures, past cultures for archaeologists and modern cultures for cultural anthropologists (also called ethnologists).

Archaeologist (also spelled archeologist): anthropologists who study culture through excavation; one of the four sub-disciplines of anthropology. Since archaeologists can't even agree on how to spell the name of their profession, you can imagine how much debate there is on such topics as why villagers around 1200 started building their homes in alcoves on Mesa Verde and why the entire northern San Juan region was abandoned around 1280.

Archaeological site: any remnant of human occupation or use such as a farming terrace, village, rock art panel, or hearth.

Architectural fabric conservator: individuals professionally trained to preserve architectural fabric such as mortar, plaster, stone, or wood.

Artifact: any portable object made by man such as a projectile point, fragment of pottery, or metate. Southwestern archaeologists are obsessed with fragments of pottery but many other objects are also uncovered during the excavation of ancestral Pueblo archaeological sites.

Atlatl: a hand-held stick used as an extension of the arm to add thrust when throwing a spear or dart.

B

Backcountry sites: sites in Mesa Verde that are not open to or viewed by the public. The management goal for these sites is to retain their scientific values.

Backfill: the process of re-covering an excavated wall or other feature of an archaeological site with dirt to return it to its pre-excavation, relatively stable condition. This is done to protect the wall or feature from the processes of erosion.

Basketmaker/Basket Maker: the term used by early explorers in the northern Southwest to designate archaeological sites that contain baskets but no pottery or only crude gray pottery. In the Pecos Classification system used by archaeologists in the northern Southwest, Basketmaker II and III are the periods which precede Pueblo I-V (see text for dates, page 6).

Belagaana: Navajo term for EuroAmerican.

Bounding wall: a free-standing wall built to define a courtyard. Typically several sides of a courtyard are defined by room walls, then a free-standing wall completes the enclosure.

C

Caliche: calcium carbonate, a natural component of desert soils and very common on Mesa Verde.

Check dam: dry-laid stones placed across a shallow drainage. The soil and moisture which builds up behind the dam makes a good location for growing domestic crops such as corn.

Chindi: Navajo term for ghost.

Chinkers (chinking stones): small stones pressed into mortar joints in walls. Very typical of Mesa Verde architecture; broken pieces of pottery (sherds) and corncobs are also sometimes used as chinkers.

Clan: a named kinship group claiming descent from a common ancestor. Depending on the culture, descent is either through the female line (matrilineal) or through the male line (patrilineal). For the Navajo, descent is through the female line so a child and his/her brothers and sisters, mother and mother's sisters and brothers are in the same clan. Clans are exogamous (one must marry outside one's own clan) so father is of a different clan. Mother's brother is an important person to a child since he is an older male of the child's clan. The Hopi, Pueblo Indians living in Arizona, also have matrilineal clans but clans are not universal among the Pueblo Indians of New Mexico. Worldwide, matrilineal clans are common for people living in small independent villages and dependent on dry farming. Consequently it is reasonable to assume that clans were present in the multi-kiva villages of Mesa Verde. But it is important to realize that a clan is NOT a residential group. A typical household would include people of more than one clan since all relatives through marriage are of a different clan.

Cliff dweller: the individuals who lived in cliff dwellings.

Cliff dwelling: more appropriately "alcove village" but the term "cliff dwelling" has been in the literature for over 100 years. A cliff dwelling is a village built in an alcove, or on a ledge in the cliff face.

Consultation group: Mesa Verde, like all federal land owning agencies, must now consult with representatives of the tribes who consider themselves descendants of the original occupants of archaeological sites. Consultant groups are taking an increasingly active interest in the management of these sites, which benefits everyone. It leads to more thoughtful management that is sensitive to the concerns of a wider range of people. The more people who know about and are interested in the preservation process the better off the resources will be.

Core and veneer: a wall construction technique in which two stone walls are built and the space between the walls is filled with dirt and small stones. This technique is one of the defining characteristics of Chaco Great House architecture. It is not that common in Mesa Verde but Sun Temple is a great example of a structure built with this type of wall.

Courtyard complex: a group of rooms in a cliff dwelling oriented around a kiva and courtyard with the kiva typically located below the floor of the courtyard. When initially built, the roof of the kiva was also the floor of the courtyard. Most kiva roofs have long since collapsed.

Cuesta: a mesa characterized by a steep escarpment on one side and a long gentle slope on the other. Mesa Verde is a very good example of a cuesta.

Culture: the sum of all learned behavior patterns shared by a group of people. This includes beliefs, customs, values, methods of providing food, shelter, and making tools. These patterns are passed from one generation to the next and can be modified through time.

Cutting dates: refers to a wood beam that retains its outer ring or bark so that a cutting date for the specimen can be determined.

D

Dado: the lower part of a wall if decorated differently from the upper part.

Deflector: a low wall placed between the hearth and ventilator shaft in a kiva. In a pithouse it is often just an upright stone placed between the hearth and vent shaft. Air entering the kiva or pithouse through the vent shaft is deflected around this feature to improve air flow in these semi- or completely subterranean rooms.

Diné: Navajo word for themselves, "the people."

Door loop: a wood loop imbedded in a wall on either side of a doorway and used to hold a stick in place that in turn holds the stone door slab in place.

Dripline: the location where water

falls as it cascades over a cliff. The natural dripline has been modified in many cliff dwelling alcoves by building berms or digging trenches on the slickrock above the alcove, or by placing a metal strip or applying a bead of silicone to the cliff face above the site.

Dry alcove: an alcove that does not contain an active spring. This is important to anyone interested in preservation, as the foundations of walls in dry alcoves have typically suffered much less water damage than those in wet alcoves.

Dry-laid stones: stones laid without mortar.

Dry-laid mudded: walls that were built by setting one stone on top of the other after which mortar was forced in the joints. Walls built in this manner are quite distinctive with the stones in contact with each other and numerous voids in the interior of the wall.

E

Extruded smoothed: a technique for finishing a mortar joint. In a wet-laid wall the mortar is allowed to over-fill a joint. Then to finish off the joint the mortar is smoothed and left to slightly protrude over the wall stones. Chinking stones (see above) are then often placed in this joint. This is the typical method of finishing mortar joints in Mesa Verde.

F

Fabric/architectural fabric: the material that is used in building walls and other features of a structure. At Mesa Verde this includes earthen mortars and plasters, sandstone blocks, and wood.

Feature: for archaeologists a general term to refer to any non-portable component of an archaeological site; as opposed to artifact which is a portable component of a site. A feature would include such things as hearths, walls, and floors.

Field house: a one- to five- or six-room structure with minimal trash and no kiva. These structures were probably built by Pueblo farmers so they could be close to their fields while their crops matured and during harvest. In times when Pueblo villages were large, field houses became very numerous. This is undoubtedly due to the fact that people living in large villages had to walk long distances to their fields. When people were more thinly scattered across the landscape they lived closer to their fields.

Front-country sites: archaeological sites in Mesa Verde which are open to the public.

H

Handhold: a man-made depression in the cliff for grasping by the hand. When there are a series of such depressions, they are termed a hand-and toehold trail by archaeologists. Such features are fairly common in the cliffs of Mesa Verde. Many depressions function as both hand-holds and toeholds.

Hearth: a defined area used for cooking or heating.

Hogan: Navajo term for "house."

I

In situ date: date from a piece of wood that is in its original location within a structure. An example would be a date from a beam that is still part of a standing wall.

Indian: the term "Indian" or "American Indian" has gone out of favor, replaced by "Native American." The Navajos on the stabilization crew, admittedly a conservative group, called themselves Indians when using a general term but primarily referred to themselves as Navajo. They definitely made a distinction between themselves as Navajos and other Indians such as Utes and Pueblos. They also made a distinction between themselves as Navajos and *anasazi*. The *anasazi*, their term, don't have sweat lodges, don't live in houses that face east, and live in villages instead of dispersed across the countryside. Ute, Pueblo Indians, and *belagaanas* have worked on the stabilization crew but with the exception of Al Lancaster, the first foreman of the crew and a *belegaana*, it is the Navajos who have devoted their entire professional lives to stabilization in Mesa Verde – some working up to 40 years on the crew.

J

Jacal: walls made with small diameter wood covered with mortar.

Jumar: a fairly small metal gadget that is designed to help??!! one ascend a climbing rope.

K

Kihu: a rectangular, surface room with many of the features of a kiva such as a bench and carefully finished interior walls. There is a kihu in Mug House.

Kiva: a Hopi term for their structures where special ceremonies take place. The term has been used by archaeologists as a label for obviously special rooms found in Ancestral Pueblo archaeological sites. In Mesa Verde these rooms typically face south or southeast and are subterranean with a keyhole shape in plan view. Features of a typical Mesa Verde kiva are southern recess, vent shaft, deflector, hearth, and six pilasters. Most kivas contain niches in their walls, have plastered walls and have a small hole in the floor just north of the hearth called a *sipapu* (see below).

L

Lithic scatter: a cluster of stone tools and/or flakes produced when making a stone tool.

Loess: wind-deposited soil, typical of the mesa top soils on Mesa Verde.

Loophole: small opening in walls; many are angled in such a way that it suggests they were used for viewing some distant area. The openings seem too small to be used for shooting arrows. The term is used in Europe to refer to holes in the walls of forts that were used for shooting and observation.

M

Matrilineal: Inheritance through the female line.

Mano and metate: mano is Spanish for hand; for an archaeologist a "mano" is a grinding tool designed to be held in the hand. The metate is the fixed stone that the mano is ground against. The mano has a convex working surface and the metate a concave working surface.

Mealing bin: during Pueblo III metates were placed in stone-lined bins called mealing bins by archaeologists. An individual would kneel at a bin, holding the mano and rubbing it against a metate. The grain would accumulate in a flat area in front of the metate.

Mealing room: a room containing one or more mealing bins. In Mesa Verde mealing bins are often found in groups of three with the surface of the metates varying from coarse to fine.

Mesa Verde: Spanish for green table; the name of a cuesta (see above) located in southwestern Colorado; also the name of a national park that encompasses a portion of the cuesta.

Metate: see mano.

Mid-country sites: a classification used to manage archaeological sites and referring to those excavated and stabilized sites that are viewed by the public but not entered by them, such as Square Tower House and Oak Tree House. Mug House, even though it is not viewed by the general public, is managed as a mid-country site.

Midden: the accumulation of human trash that is inevitably associated with a dwelling or village. Middens in Mesa Verde include pieces of broken pottery, discarded stone tools, bones of such animals as deer and rabbit, and often human burials.

Moiety: one of two divisions found in some societies; the divisions can be based on kinship (such as clans belong to one or the other division) but this is not always the case. Several of the Pueblo groups in New Mexico are divided into summer and winter people or in some Pueblos they are called pumpkin and turquoise people.

P

Pecked-face architecture: walls made up of stones shaped by pecking, a standard finishing technique during the Pueblo III period on Mesa Verde.

Pecos Conference: an annual gathering of Southwest archaeologists where new discoveries and ideas are discussed; the first conference was in 1927 at Pecos Pueblo in New Mexico. The classification system developed at the first Pecos Conference for ancestral Pueblo archaeological sites is still the standard used in the northern San Juan area of the Southwest.

Petroglyph: rock art pecked, carved or ground on stone.

Pictograph: rock art that is painted on natural stone or walls.

Pithouse: a subsurface dwelling used by the ancestral Pueblos from about 600 to 900 on Mesa Verde. Through time the pithouse became more specialized and is then termed a kiva (900 to 1300) by archaeologists.

Plan map: a bird's-eye view of an archaeological site.

Portland cement: a cement that hardens under water, first used by the Romans.

Provenience: origin or original location of an object.

R

Re-point: to add new mortar to an eroded mortar joint.

Rock art: an image on rock; images can be produced by pecking, grinding, scratching, or painting a stone surface.

Roof fall: in discussions of alcoves, this is the stone material that is found when a section of the alcove roof is dislodged and falls on the surface below. Needless to say, damage can be done to anything impacted by this material.

Room block: a group of rooms that are connected by common walls.

Room suite: three to nine interconnected rooms with some adjacent outdoor space; typically there is one living room which is connected by doorway to several storage rooms; several suites and a kiva make up a courtyard unit.

Room racks: a series of parallel, small diameter wood beams, several feet apart, which extend across a room at about waist level. Two rooms in Balcony House contain room racks.

Ruin: an abandoned structure. In the late 1980s and early 1990s, the museum and other historic buildings were receiving all kinds of project funds for new roofs, replacement of windows, etc., and the archaeological sites for which the park was established were being ignored in park service budgets. One response was to convince the park service that the cliff dwellings and mesa top sites were also buildings that needed attention. So the term "ruin" was replaced with house, as in Far View House, and Ruins Road was changed to the Mesa Top Loop. An effort was also made to get the cliff dwellings and other structures with standing walls listed on the National Park Service's List of Classified Structures: a list of all structures in the National Park Service. This happened in the late 1990s.

S

Salvage archaeology: excavations that are necessitated because an archaeological site is to be destroyed, typically by some construction project; erosion can also necessitate salvage archaeology.

Sandstone-shale contact: the contact where porous sandstone and less porous shale meet. This often results in a spring or seep; the natural alcoves of Mesa Verde are typically found in these contact zones.

Scupper: a trough placed so as to move the flow of water away from a cliff or wall.

Sipapu: a Hopi word; a small hole in the floor of kivas and pithouses that symbolizes the place of emergence from the underworld; placed in line with and north of the fire pit, deflector, vent shaft complex.

Site fabric: the material that was used to build the walls and features of an archaeological site. In a cliff dwelling this would be earthen mortars and plasters, stones, and wood.

Skinwalker: a witch that dresses up in the skin of a coyote or wolf.

Sootu: the Hopi word for the Milky Way.

Slish: the Navajo word for dirt. Also the word for mortar.

Society: a group of people that interact regularly and share a culture.

Spall rock: pieces of sandstone detaching from the roof of an alcove and falling on walls, trails, and courtyards below. The term also refers to spalls removed when shaping construction stone or flakes that detach after sandstone is heated.

Stabilization: the activities that go into making an archaeological site stable. This can be anything from hoeing weeds to diverting water to replacing deteriorated stones in a wall. The terms stabilization, preservation, and conservation have faded in and out of favor in the past 50 or so years. but refer to the same process. It is important to note that currently proper stabilization demands complete documentation.

Storage cist: a subsurface pit specifically for storage; found in association with pithouses.

Stratigraphy: the layering of soil, rocks, artifacts, etc.; used to determine the relative age of the deposits.

T

Talus: a sloping pile of rocks at the base of a cliff.

Tchamahia: a Hopi term; a very finely made stone hoe used in special ceremonies.

To: the Navajo word for water.

Toehold: a man-made depression specifically for the foot. A series of such depressions is called a hand- and toehold trail. In fact there is no way to distinguish depressions for the hand or foot except location and on many trails depressions function for both hands and feet.

Tower: at Mesa Verde a tower is an above-ground circular room; typically towers have double-course walls and few floor features. On mesa top sites many are connected to a kiva by a tunnel. The "tower" of painted tower in Cliff Palace and the "tower" of Square Tower House are in fact not towers but roomblocks, but Cliff Palace and many cliff dwellings do contain towers. There are two in Spruce Tree House. In Hovenweep National Monument towers can be square, circular, or D-shaped, with Square Tower and Round Tower examples of towers in the Square Tower Group of buildings.

Transhumance: a seasonal round of movement for people (and livestock).

Treatment: the process and materials used to make a wall or other feature stable.

Tse: the Navajo word for stone.

Tumpline: a strap placed against the head or chest to help support a pack carried on a person's back.

Type site: an archaeological site selected because it contains features standard to sites of that type so it functions as an example. Spruce Tree House was Fewkes' "type" cliff dwelling.

U

Unit pueblo: a standard building unit on the Colorado Plateau with storage and living rooms, kiva and midden constructed on a north-south or northwest-southeast axis.

V

Vent shaft: a shaft leading from the ground surface into a pithouse or kiva to facilitate the flow of fresh air.

W

Wall abutment: one wall butting up against another wall. This can be a key to the relative date of construction of the walls.

Wall niche: a small recess in a wall. Niches are common in the walls of kivas and are sometimes found in room walls.

Water reservoir: a man-made feature designed to hold water. There is one on exhibit in the Far View area.

Wet alcove: an active spring is located within the alcove.

Wet-laid: during wall construction stones are laid on a bed of mortar.

Y

Yeibichai: Navajo divinities; they are represented by masked dancers in Navajo ceremonies; Yei figures are woven into rugs, found on Navajo rock art panels and represented on sandpaintings.

ADDENDA

The staff who worked with Kathy Fiero from 1983 to 2002.

MASONRY WORKERS:
Lon Ayers, Raymond Begay, Willie Begay, Allen Brown, Bill Dale, James Frank, Lewis Joe, Mark Johannsen, Arnold John, Kee Charley John, Robert Orlando, Harold Peshlakai, Neill Smith, Mike Suglia, Gene Trujillo, Bob Yusten

ARCHAEOLOGISTS/ARCHAEO TECHS:
George Arms, Julie Bell, Joel Brisbin, Maureen Cavanaugh, Mark Dean, Liz Francisco, Noreen Fritz, Jim Hampson, Dave Johnson, Vince McMillan, Wayne NeeSmith, Cynthia Williams, Phil Wilson

MUSEUM TECHS:
Anita Vialpando, Deborah Kelly Galin

TREE-RING LAB STAFF IN PARK:
Rex Adams, Laura Baxter, Jeff Dean, Jim Parks, James Riser, David Street, Ron Towner, Dick Warren

ROCK ART DOCUMENTATION CREW:
Ken Benson, Karen Borger, Sheri Bowman, Laurel Casjens, Charles Cole, Sally Cole, Leslie David, Lena DeTar, Sylvia DeTar, Grant Fahrni, Carole Graham, Charles Hardy, Victoria Jefferies, Wilton Kooyahoema, Laura Lantz, Leroy Lewis, Stacey Monty, Gilbert Naseyowma, Laura Ninneman, Harold Polingyumptewa, Raleigh Puhuyaoma, Morgan Saufkie, Jim Tawyesva, Dalton Taylor, Myers Walker

PLASTER PRESERVATION CREW:
Veronica Aplenc, Maribel Beas, Brynn Bender, Linda Berger, Elsa Bourginon, Claudia Cancino, Rebecca Carr, Chris Carson, Carla Cielo, Elisa del Bono, Amanda Didden, Enrico DiNicola, Scott Doyle, Linnea Dix, Kate Dowdy, Rosanne Dube, Elisabeth Dubin, Ana Maria Duran, Julie Eklund, David Facenda, Marie Farneth, John Fidler, Caroline Finch, Karen Fix, Kecia Fong, Kathleen Forest, Rynta Fourie, Joshua Freedland, Chris Frey, Mark Goodman, Sarah Gray, Mary Hardy, Monica Harter, Bob Hartzler, Carolyn Hesse, Amy Cole Ives, Renee Jones, Jocelyn Kimmel, Barry Knight, Evan Kopelson, Dorothy Krotzer, Molly Lambert, Pietro Mangarella, Frank Matero, Lisa McCormack, Kate McDowell, Lorraine McVey, Lauren Meyer, Sarah Meyer, Christine Miller, Judi Moon, David Myers, Antje Neumenn, Anne Oliver, Ayzegul Ozer, Al Parker, Jay Platt, Judy Peters, Brad Roeder, Alvin Romancito, Averil Ramirez, Angelyn Bass Rivera, Larry Sisson, Mary Slater, Jessica Sloop, Pushkar Sohoni, Nicholas Stapp, Jerry Strickler, Christeen Taniguchi, Jeanne Marie Teutonico, Preston Thayer, Evin Tobin, Sibylla Tringham, Catherine Turton, Nuanlak Watsantachad, Jean Wolf

SUGGESTIONS FOR FURTHER READING

Al Lancaster's private collection of notebooks, books, and photos is housed at the Center of Southwest Studies, Fort Lewis College, Durango, Colorado. A large collection of Nusbaum photographs is in the Photo Archives of the Museum of New Mexico, Santa Fe, and his private collection of letters and notes is in the Anthropological Archives of the Natural History Museum, Smithsonian, Washington, D.C., with a small collection in the Research Center, Mesa Verde National Park.

FOR THOSE INTERESTED IN LEARNING MORE

A general book on Southwestern archaeology:
Cordell, Linda S.
    1997   *Archaeology of the Southwest,* Academic Press.

One recently published book on the ancestral Pueblos:
Kantner, John
    2004   *Ancient Puebloan Southwest,* Cambridge University Press.

Site reports on the cliff dwellings of Mesa Verde:
Cattanach, George S.
    1980   *Long House,* Publications in Archaeology 7H. National Park Service. Washington.
Fewkes, Jesse W.
    1909   *Antiquities of the Mesa Verde National Park, Spruce Tree House,* Bureau of American Ethnology, Bulletin 41. Washington.
    1911   *Antiquities of the Mesa Verde National Park, Cliff Palace,* Bureau of American Ethnology, Bulletin 51. Washington.
Fiero, Kathleen
    1999   *Balcony House: A History of a Cliff Dwelling,* Archaeological Research Series, No. 8-A. Mesa Verde Museum Association.
Nordby, Larry
    2001   *Prelude to Tapestries in Stone: Understanding Cliff Palace Architecture,* Archaeological Research Series Architectural Studies Number 4. Mesa Verde National Park Division of Research and Resource Management.

Nordenskiöld, Gustaf
   1893   *The Cliff Dwellers of the Mesa Verde, Southwestern
           Colorado, Their Pottery and Implements,* Trans. By D.
           Lloyd Morgan. P.A. Norstedt & Soner, Stockholm-Chicago.

Rohn, Arthur H.
   1971   *Mug House,* Archaeological Research Series, No. 7-D.
           National Park Service. Washington.

A great overview of the history of archaeology in the Four Corners region:
   Lister, Florence
      2004   *Troweling Through Time: The First Century of Mesa
              Verdean Archaeology,* University of New Mexico Press,
              Albuquerque.

And for those who want something on the lighter side:
   A mystery set in Mesa Verde National Park:
   Barr, Nevada
      1995   *Ill Wind,* Putnam.

On mysteries set on the Navajo Reservation:
   Hillerman, Tony (many but my favorites)
      1973   *Dance Hall of the Dead,* Harper & Row.
      1988   *A Thief of Time,* Harper & Row.

   Aimee and David Thurlo (Ella Clah mysteries)
      2005   *White Thunder,* Forge.

INDEX